SCHOLASTIC

P9-CLC-539

Independent Reading Management Kit:
Literary Elements

Michele L. McCaughtry

New York • Toronto • London • Auckland • Sydney
Mexico City • New Delhi • Hong Kong • Buenos Aires

Teaching Resources

DEDICATION

This book is dedicated to the students at South Range Local School District whose bright minds and caring hearts inspire me daily.

To my fellow colleagues for their ideas, support, and enthusiasm.

To my husband, Keith for his support and encouragement along the way.

To my daughters, Ainsley and Alexa, who took three hour naps so that this dream could become a reality.

To my friends and family, especially my mom, dad, and mother-in-law who agreed to watch the kids so I can get in just one more page.

CREDITS

Activities and art for pages 33 and 63 adapted from *Origami Math: Grades 2–3* and *Origami Math: Grades 4–6*
© by Karen Baicker, 2004.
Published by Scholastic Inc. Used with permission.

Cover design by Brian LaRossa
Interior design by Solutions by Design, Inc.

ISBN-13: 978-0-439-64043-5
ISBN-10: 0-439-64043-1

2 3 4 5 6 7 8 9 10   40   12 11 10 09 08 07

Table of Contents

INTRODUCTION

The purpose of this book is to provide teachers of grades 4 to 8 with a way to help their students become more independent and responsible readers. I've found that the best way to achieve this with my own middle school students is to teach each reading objective well and then give students a choice of activities. When students are given a choice in their own learning, they feel a sense of ownership; they take control and set a purpose for completing the assignment.

One of my favorite ways to provide choices for reading-response activities is to design a Think-Tac-Toe grid full of projects—a choice board for learning. For each of the seven literary elements covered in this book, you'll find a Think-Tac-Toe grid that lists nine engaging projects for students to complete during independent work time. Students choose which projects they want to complete according to their individual strengths and learning-style preferences (written, oral, visual, and/or kinesthetic). Each project comes with an easy-to-follow assignment sheet that guides students to completion; students can set their own pace while working on their projects and you can assist students as needed.

Most important, this independent reading management kit offers a student-centered way to differentiate your instruction for all learners: Your reluctant readers will enjoy completing activities that are within their comfort zone and your above-average readers will soar with activities that require more in-depth thinking.

How to Use This Book

The projects in this book may be used as an independent reading program or they may be used to supplement your existing program. Each chapter presents nine project options in a Think-Tac-Toe grid to help students explore a specific literary element. The projects come with student-friendly instructions and grading criteria to help guide them and enable you and your students to easily evaluate their work.

How you decide to use the project choices will depend on your teaching style, your classroom setup, and how much independent work your students are able to handle. Here are a few different ways you can structure the work:

- As an independent study on a certain literary element.

- As an end-of-the-novel project or after reading a few chapters to assess what students have learned so far about one or more literary elements.

- As a way to have students practice reading response using several literary elements you would like them to focus on.

- As a tiered assignment.

- To offer both teacher- and student-choice assignments.

- To encourage critical thinking through teacher- and student-created assignments.

Independent Study

If you choose to conduct an independent study on a literary element, have students review the assigned Think-Tac-Toe grid and decide on three projects to complete after they've finished a novel. Then have students complete and sign a contract that lists their project choices (see the reproducible contract on page 8). In this way, students know what you expect and understand how to reach that expectation. Make sure that both you and their parent or guardian review and sign the contract so that everyone is held accountable: the teacher, the student, and the parent.

Have students use the Daily Log on page 9 to set goals for themselves as they work independently in class. (I have my students note the work they've finished on the form and turn it in everyday before they leave my class so I can initial it and keep track of their progress.)

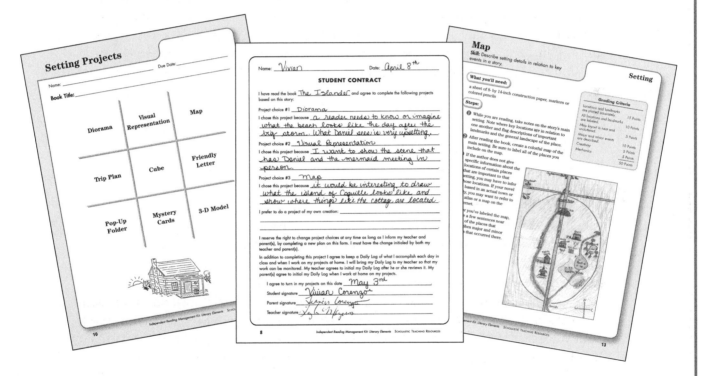

End-of-Novel Assessment

When they've finished a novel, give the whole class the same Think-Tac-Toe grid to complete and let students select project choices for the literary element.

If students need more scaffolding, have them complete just one assignment from the Think-Tac-Toe grid after reading a few chapters of the novel. For example, recently I had my entire class read the first four chapters of Robert C. O'Brien's *Mrs. Frisby and the Rats of NIMH* and then choose one reading-response project according to their interests and strengths. I assigned the setting Think-Tac-Toe grid (page 10), because the novel covered much of the setting in these chapters. I used the project grade in place of a quiz on setting.

Combined-Literary-Element Instruction

If you would like to have students focus on more than one element at a time, you can create a Think-Tac-Toe grid that targets multiple literary elements by cutting and pasting sections of different literary element pages on to the blank Think-Tac-Toe grid on page 112.

Have students choose a project from each row so they work on all the literary elements you've selected. For example, if you have students who need practice in the areas of characterization, setting, and point of view, then you may give them a multiple-literary-element Think-Tac-Toe to work on, as shown in the example.

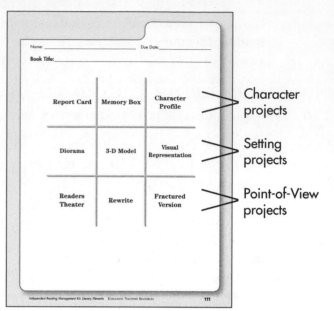

Differentiated Assignments

You can create differentiated learning tasks by assigning students the appropriate Think-Tac-Toe grid. For example, you may have six students working on projects from the plot grid, while five are working on the theme grid.

You also may want to have students who need more support complete only one project from the grid, while you assign two or more projects to students who require a more challenging assignment. This leveled option works well for a mixed-ability classroom.

Teacher- and Student-Choice Assignments

Another way to use the Think-Tac-Toe grid is to select a teacher-choice project that students must complete and circle it on the grid—or create your own assignment and write it in the center of the grid. (I usually write this project in the middle square and label it "Teacher's Choice." Students know that they are all responsible for completing that project.) Let students choose one or two more projects from the remaining options. This format encourages students to take control of their own learning while allowing you to assess all students on a single project that targets a specific learning goal.

> **Tip**
>
> Almost all projects require paper and pencil or pen. Additional materials are listed for each project. Be sure to have a supply of both lined and unlined (copy) paper available for your students.

Teacher- or Student-Created Assignments

When students are familiar with the Think-Tac-Toe grid format, you may want to create your own grid to teach other reading objectives. Fill in a copy of the blank grid template with your own project choices. For example, you may design an assignment grid that focuses on a certain novel, author's craft, and more.

Students also may want to create their own Think-Tac-Toe assignment grids. Encourage them to develop a set of activities around a specific literary element or reading objective.

Introducing Independent Reading Activities for Literary Elements

After I've taught a new literary element, I make an overhead transparency of the Think-Tac-Toe board for that element and a set of copies for the class. I show the transparency on the overhead and give a brief summary of each project. I ask students to put stars next to the projects they may want to do. Then I invite them to attend an informational meeting on the projects they've starred. At the meeting, I hand out copies of the activity directions, review the procedures, and answer any questions. After they've attended several meetings, I give them one day to narrow their choices to three projects, fill in the Student Contract, and have it signed.

Every day before they work on the project in class, I expect students to set goals for what they will accomplish. At the end of the period they record what they actually have accomplished in their Daily Logs. I collect the logs before students leave and, later, review and initial them, so I can monitor their progress each day.

Assessing Student Work

Each project has its own rubric with specific grading criteria. Students can use the rubric on their project direction sheet for guidance. At the end of each chapter, you'll find a grading summary sheet that includes the rubrics for the nine projects. Make a copy of the summary sheet for each student and check the boxes next to the three projects he or she decides to complete. Grade the projects as the student completes them. When the student has completed all three, record the final total on the summary line at the bottom. This score will be his or her final grade.

Displaying Student Work

Once all three projects have been turned in and graded, I choose some examples of outstanding work to display around the room and out in the hallway. I think it is important for students to see what other projects look like. It also motivates students to preview projects they may have a chance to work on soon.

Name: _____ Date: _____

STUDENT CONTRACT

I have read the book _____ and agree to complete the following projects based on this story:

Project choice #1 _____

I chose this project because _____

_____

_____.

Project choice #2 _____

I chose this project because _____

_____

_____.

Project choice #3 _____

I chose this project because _____

_____

_____.

I prefer to do a project of my own creation: _____

_____

_____.

I reserve the right to change project choices at any time as long as I inform my teacher and parent(s), by completing a new plan on this form. I must have the change initialed by both my teacher and parent(s).

In addition to completing this project I agree to keep a Daily Log of what I accomplish each day in class and when I work on my projects at home. I will bring my Daily Log to my teacher so that my work can be monitored. My teacher agrees to initial my Daily Log after he or she reviews it. My parent(s) agree to initial my Daily Log when I work at home on my projects.

I agree to turn in my projects on this date _____.

Student signature _____

Parent signature _____

Teacher signature _____

Name: _____ Date: _____

DAILY LOG

Date:	Goals I plan to achieve today:	Goals I actually accomplished today:	Teacher Initials

Setting Projects

Name: _____ Due Date: _____

Book Title: _____

Diorama	**3-D Model**	**Visual Representation**
Map	**Trip Plan**	**Cube**
Friendly Letter	**Pop-Up Folder**	**Mystery Cards**

Independent Reading Management Kit: Literary Elements   SCHOLASTIC TEACHING RESOURCES

Diorama

Skill: Represent a setting that is important to the plot.

What you'll need:

shoe box, craft materials, glue, scissors, markers or paints

Steps:

❶ Select a key scene from the book you've read in which the setting is important to the plot.

❷ Inside the box create a diorama of the scene using craft materials. Keep in mind the place, time period, environmental details such as weather, and the characters in the scene. Consider how these factors change or are changed by the setting. Make sure you cover the inside of the box completely.

❸ On a sheet of paper write two or three paragraphs that describe the scene you depicted, how the setting is important to the story development, and why you chose that scene for your project.

Grading Criteria	
Diorama focuses on a single scene.	5 Points
Artwork accurately depicts the setting.	15 Points
Artwork is neat and colorful.	5 Points
Write-up includes all elements in Step 3.	20 Points
Mechanics	5 Points
	50 Points

3-D Model

Skill: Replicate setting details using creative materials.

What you'll need:

Map Project activity sheet (page 13), foam board or cardboard for model base, clay, construction paper, craft materials (odds and ends)

Steps:

❶ Follow the steps given for the map project, except make the map into a 3-D model, using a sheet of foam board or cardboard as your building base.

❷ Make sure you create your model to scale. For example, trees should be taller than people.

Grading Criteria	
Locations and landmarks are placed accurately.	10 Points
3-D items are effective and to scale.	10 Points
All locations and landmarks are labeled.	5 Points
Map layout is neat and uncluttered.	5 Points
Major and minor events are described.	10 Points
Creativity	5 Points
Mechanics	5 Points
	50 Points

Visual Representation

Skill: Artistically depict a scene that affected you emotionally.

What you'll need:

any art medium such as clay, paper, or watercolors (or a combination of art media), glue or tape, and How to Write a Cinquain Poem (page 18)

Steps:

1 Review the book you've read and choose a scene to which you had a strong emotional response.

2 Use your artistic strength to create this scene in the art medium of your choice.

3 After you complete the artwork, use the how-to guide to create a cinquain poem that describes your scene and how it affected you emotionally.

4 Cut out your poem and attach it to your visual representation.

Grading Criteria

Artwork is detailed and accurately depicts the setting.	20 Points
Cinquain poem uses correct cinquain form.	5 Points
Cinquain poem accurately depicts setting.	5 Points
Cinquain poem depicts emotional feelings.	5 Points
Mechanics	5 Points
Creativity	5 Points
Layout	5 Points
	50 Points

Cinquain for "Bound for Oregon"

Oregon
Rich land, food shortages
Traveling, building, storing
Hardships along the way
Journey

Map

Skill: Describe setting details in relation to key events in a story.

What you'll need:

a sheet of 8- by 14-inch construction paper, markers or colored pencils

Steps:

1 While you are reading, take notes on the story's main setting. Note where key locations are in relation to one another and flag descriptions of important landmarks and the general landscape of the place.

2 After reading the book, create a colorful map of the main setting. Be sure to label all of the places you include on the map.

3 If the author does not give specific information about the locations of certain places that are important to that setting, you may have to infer those locations. If your novel is based in an actual town or city, you may want to refer to an atlas or a map on the Internet.

4 After you've labeled the map, write a few sentences near each of the places that describes major and minor events that occurred there.

Grading Criteria

Locations and landmarks are placed accurately.	15 Points
All locations and landmarks are labeled.	10 Points
Map layout is neat and uncluttered.	5 Points
Major and minor events are described.	10 Points
Creativity	5 Points
Mechanics	5 Points
	50 Points

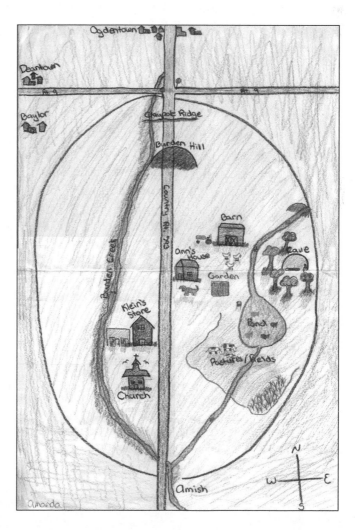

Trip Plan

Skill: Develop a real or fictional setting that matches a character's personality traits.

What you'll need:

construction paper, markers, colored pencils, and any other items that will add to the creativity of your project

Steps:

1 Pretend that you are a travel agent and your job is to send the main character from the book you've read on a trip. You will need to plan the entire trip for your client and present him or her with a complete packet of documents for the trip.

2 Think about a trip you feel would suit the main character. It could be a trip the character actually took in the story (a real location or a fictional location the author has described). Think about this character's traveling preferences, activities, or interests, and any experience he or she has had traveling.

3 After selecting the destination, you may start assembling the documents your character will need for the trip. You may include five or more of the items listed below:

- Map
- Passport
- Coupons
- Itinerary
- Driver's license
- Info pamphlets
- Plane/bus/train
- Tickets to special events/attractions
- Motel/hotel vouchers
- Helpful hints
- Anything else you can think of

4 Make a folder out of construction paper and title it "Travel Plans for _name of character_." Add appropriate decorations to the outside.

5 On the back of the folder write two to three paragraphs that answer these questions:
- What aspects of the character's personality made you send him or her to this place
- What would the main character like about the location?

6 Place all documents necessary for the trip inside the folder.

Grading Criteria

Trip is appropriate for the character.	15 Points
Five or more items are placed in folder.	10 Points
Work is neat and colorful.	5 Points
Explanation of trip plan answers questions in Step 5.	10 Points
Creativity	5 Points
Mechanics	5 Points
	50 Points

Cube

Skill: Identify key aspects of a setting.

What you'll need:

Cube Template (page 19), construction paper, scissors, glue, colored pencils or markers

Steps:

1 After reading the book, analyze the different aspects of the setting listed below.

2 Use the cube template to create your setting cube.
Before you cut it out, illustrate and write the following on each side:
- Side 1: Author's name and title of book
- Side 2: Where the story took place
- Side 3: When the story took place
- Side 4: The mood conveyed throughout the story (how the setting made you feel)
- Side 5: Connections you made between the setting and another text, your own experience, or with an experience you may have read about or seen
- Side 6: Other books by this author and the main setting of each

3 Cut out the template and glue the sides of the cube together.

Grading Criteria	
Sides of cube are designed according to the criteria in Step 2.	15 Points
All sides of cube are well illustrated.	10 Points
Descriptions make sense.	10 Points
Entire cube is neat and colorful.	15 Points
	50 Points

Friendly Letter

Skill: Use sensory detail to describe a setting.

What you'll need:

Friendly Letter Checklist (page 20)

Steps:

1 Pretend you are a character from the book you've read and you are writing a friendly letter to another character in the story or a character you invent. In this letter you will describe your living conditions and the setting that surrounds you on a daily basis.

2 Describe as many aspects as you can using sensory details. Sensory details are what you can see, hear, smell, taste, and touch.

3 When drafting your letter, use the checklist.

4 Design a letterhead, envelope, and stamp that reflect the setting of your novel. Write or type your final copy of your letter on this letterhead. The envelope must follow correct address format.

Grading Criteria	
Letter reflects characters' surroundings using sensory details.	15 Points
It follows friendly-letter format.	10 Points
Letterhead, stamp, envelope reflect setting.	15 Points
Envelope is addressed correctly.	10 points
	50 Points

Pop-Up Folder

Skill: Show how the setting can reflect the message or theme of a story.

What you'll need:

letter-size manila file folder or oaktag, ruler, construction paper, markers or colored pencils, glue, scissors, tissue paper, cellophane, or other items that will add to the creativity of your project

Steps:

❶ Choose a scene from the book you've read that you feel best depicts the message or theme of the story.

❷ Create a pop-up folder of this scene, using the directions listed below.

❸ Make sure you include exact elements of the setting that were described in the scene (trees, landmarks, pastures, etc.).

❹ Make sure that when the entire scene is done, you have completely filled up the background of the file folder so that you cannot tell it was a file folder.

❺ On the back of the file folder include a short write-up that describes what is happening in this particular scene, the setting that is being depicted, and the message the setting is conveying to the readers.

POP-UP FOLDER DIRECTIONS

1. Fold the oaktag in half and make a smooth, even crease.
2. If you would like to change the background color of the oaktag, cover it with colored construction paper.
3. Use a ruler to draw the three or four tabs on which you will glue each item that pops up. The tabs should be at least 1 inch long and about $1/2$ inch wide.
4. Cut the tabs by making slits along the lines you drew.
5. Open the folded oaktag. Pull the tabs inside and crease the fold to make the folder stand open.
6. Illustrate and cut out pop-up pieces that show important elements of the setting of the book. Glue the pieces onto the tabs. (Keep in mind not to use too many pop-up items; it could be distracting and take away from the effect. Make no more than four pieces.)
7. Color the background or illustrate it to add scenic details around the pop-up pieces.
8. Make sure your write-up appears on the back of the pop-up folder.

Grading Criteria

Pop-up folder effectively represents setting.	10 Points
Pictures actually pop up out of the folder.	10 Points
Layout is neat and uncluttered.	10 Points
Pop-up folder is colored appropriately.	10 Points
Write-up includes three elements listed in Step 5.	10 Points
	50 Points

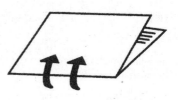

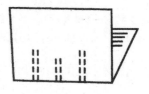

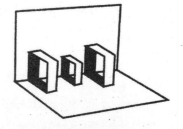

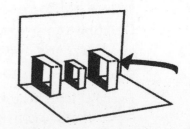

Mystery Cards

Skill: Use higher-level thinking to infer the aspects of the setting.

What you'll need:

10 unlined index cards

Steps:

❶ Make index cards for ten different aspects of the setting, such as important places, landmarks, or dates. These mystery cards will give clues so other readers can guess the aspects you have chosen.

❷ On the front of each card, write two or three clues that reveal the aspect of the setting. The clues can be given in written or symbolic form. On the back of the card, write the answer with a detailed explanation.

❸ The cards must have enough information to reveal the aspect of the setting, without giving it away.

Grading Criteria	
Ten cards are completed with unique setting mysteries.	5 Points
Each card lists two to three clues.	5 Points
Clues are appropriate.	15 Points
Creativity of the entire card	10 Points
Neatness (layout and color)	10 Points
Mechanics	5 Points
	50 Points

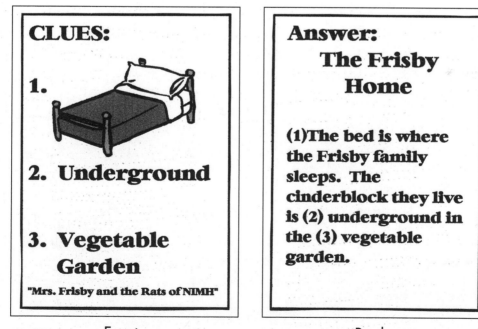

CLUES:

1.

2. Underground

3. Vegetable Garden

"Mrs. Frisby and the Rats of NIMH"

Answer:
The Frisby Home

(1) The bed is where the Frisby family sleeps. The cinderblock they live is (2) underground in the (3) vegetable garden.

Front   Back

HOW TO WRITE A CINQUAIN POEM

To write a cinquain poem, follow this pattern:

Noun
Adjective, adjective
Verb+ing, verb+ing, verb+ing
Four-word free statement
Synonym

Example:

Poem written in response to *Flowers for Algernon* by Daniel Keyes

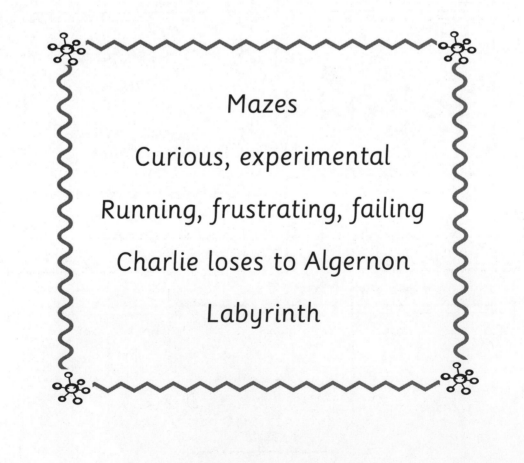

Mazes

Curious, experimental

Running, frustrating, failing

Charlie loses to Algernon

Labyrinth

CUBE TEMPLATE

Cut out the template around the outline below. Fold along the dotted lines and shape into a cube. Glue and secure the flaps.

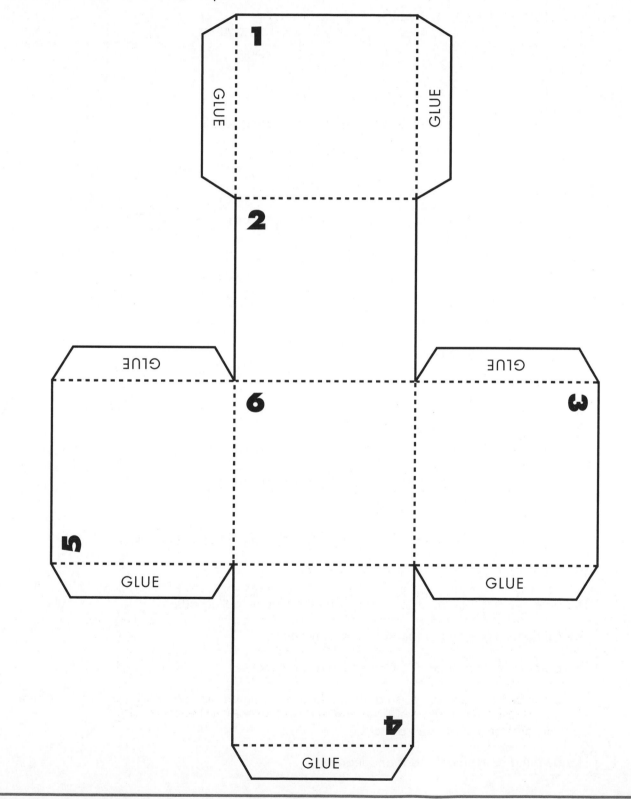

Name: _____   Date: _____

FRIENDLY LETTER CHECKLIST

Your address
Date   ← Heading

Salutation
or   →   Dear _____,
Greeting

The body of the letter: This is where you express your
thoughts and ideas. Basically, it communicates why you are
writing the letter.   → Body

Be sure to indent the first line of every paragraph and
leave lines between paragraphs.

Closing   →   Love, *or* Yours truly,

_____
Your signature

Before turning in your letter, proofread it carefully, following the checklist below:

☐ Your address is given in full in the upper right.

☐ The date is placed in the upper right, with the month spelled out.

☐ The salutation/greeting is followed by a comma.

☐ The paragraphs are indented and separated by spaces.

☐ The first word of the closing is capitalized, and the entire closing is followed by a comma.

☐ Spelling and grammar are correct.

☐ Handwriting or typing is neat and legible.

Name: _____ Date: _____

GRADING SUMMARY

	Possible Score:	My Score:

☐ **Diorama**

	Possible Score:	My Score:
Diorama focuses on a single scene.	5 Points	_____
Artwork accurately depicts the setting.	15 Points	_____
Artwork is neat and colorful.	5 Points	_____
Write-up includes all elements in Step 3.	20 Points	_____
Mechanics	5 Points	_____
	50 Points	_____

☐ **3-D Model**

	Possible Score	My Score
Locations and landmarks are placed accurately.	10 Points	_____
3-D items are effective and to scale.	10 Points	_____
All locations/landmarks are labeled.	5 Points	_____
Map layout is neat and uncluttered.	5 Points	_____
Major and minor events are described.	10 Points	_____
Creativity	5 Points	_____
Mechanics	5 Points	_____
	50 Points	_____

☐ **Visual Representation**

	Possible Score	My Score
Artwork is detailed and accurately depicts the setting.	20 Points	_____
Cinquain poem uses correct cinquain form.	5 Points	_____
Cinquain poem accurately depicts setting.	5 Points	_____
Cinquain poem depicts emotional feelings.	5 Points	_____
Mechanics	5 Points	_____
Creativity	5 Points	_____
Layout	5 Points	_____
	50 Points	_____

☐ **Map**

	Possible Score	My Score
Locations and landmarks are placed accurately.	15 Points	_____
All locations and landmarks are labeled.	10 Points	_____
Map layout is neat and uncluttered.	5 Points	_____
Major and minor events are described.	10 Points	_____
Creativity	5 Points	_____
Mechanics	5 Points	_____
	50 Points	_____

☐ Trip Plan

Trip is appropriate for the character.	15 Points	_____
Five or more items are placed in folder.	10 Points	_____
Work is neat and colorful.	5 Points	_____
Explanation of trip plan answers questions in Step 5.	10 Points	_____
Creativity	5 Points	_____
Mechanics	5 Points	_____
	50 Points	_____

☐ Cube

Sides of cube are designed according to the criteria in Step 2.	15 Points	_____
All sides of cube are well illustrated.	10 Points	_____
Descriptions make sense.	10 Points	_____
Entire cube is neat and colorful.	15 Points	_____
	50 Points	_____

☐ Friendly Letter

Letter reflects characters' surroundings using sensory details.	15 Points	_____
It follows friendly letter format.	10 Points	_____
Letterhead, stamp, envelope reflect setting.	15 Points	_____
Envelope is addressed correctly.	10 points	_____
	50 Points	_____

☐ Pop-Up Folder

Pop-up folder effectively represents setting.	10 Points	_____
Pictures actually pop up out of the folder.	10 Points	_____
Layout is neat and uncluttered.	10 Points	_____
Pop-up folder is colored appropriately.	10 Points	_____
Write-up includes three elements listed in Step 5.	10 Points	_____
	50 Points	_____

☐ Mystery Cards

Ten cards are completed with unique setting mysteries.	5 Points	_____
Each card lists two to three clues.	5 Points	_____
Clues are appropriate.	15 Points	_____
Creativity of the entire card	10 Points	_____
Neatness (layout and color)	10 Points	_____
Mechanics	5 Points	_____
	50 Points	_____

Total for all three projects _____

Independent Reading Management Kit: Literary Elements   SCHOLASTIC TEACHING RESOURCES

Plot Projects

Name: _____   Due Date: _____

Book Title: _____

Chart	**Scrapbook**	**Plot Picture**
Clay Model	**Yearbook**	**Cube**
Puppet Show	**Paper Chain**	**Mini-Picture Book**

Chart

Skill: Identify the five plot elements in a story.

What you'll need:

a 9- by 12-inch sheet of construction paper, colored pencils, ruler, Plotline Guidelines (page 31)

Steps:

❶ Divide the sheet of construction paper into eight separate blocks. Organize and label each block as follows:

- Block 1: Title of book and author
- Block 2: Introduction (setting)
- Block 3: Introduction (characters)
- Block 4: Introduction (main problem in the story)
- Block 5: Rising action
- Block 6: Climax
- Block 7: Falling action
- Block 8: Conclusion

❷ Review the book you've read to determine the characters, the setting, and the five plot elements described in the Plotline Guidelines.

❸ In each block on your chart, draw a scene from the book that illustrates the appropriate element.

❹ Under each illustration write a caption to explain how the scene you chose corresponds with the title, setting, characters, or plot point.

Grading Criteria	
Chart accurately represents all five plot elements from the book.	15 Points
Artwork is neat and colorful.	10 Points
Captions describe the pictures well.	15 Points
Mechanics	5 Points
Creativity	5 Points
	50 Points

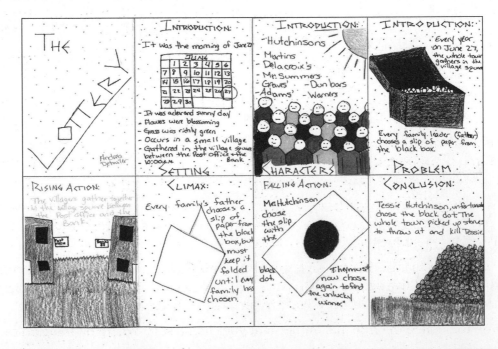

Scrapbook

Skill: Synthesize information about the story's plot in a scrapbook format.

What you'll need:

five sheets of construction paper, Plotline Guidelines (page 31), colored pencils or markers, scissors, stapler, glue, craft materials to add to the page

Steps:

❶ Make a unique scrapbook page for each of the five plot elements (see the guidelines for a description of the elements.)

❷ At the top of each page, write the name of the plot element ("Introduction," "Rising Action," etc.)

❸ In the middle of each page, arrange and paste pictures and other creative items that correspond to the plot element. Feel free to use stickers, clip art, 3-D items, and other craft materials, but remember to stay focused on the plot element you're illustrating.

❹ At the bottom of each page, write a short caption explaining how the collage you made describes the plot element.

❺ Staple or otherwise bind the pages together to make a booklet.

Grading Criteria

Scrapbook accurately displays all plot elements.	15 Points
Scrapbook is creative, colorful, and laid out well.	15 Points
A written explanation of the scrapbook is included on each page.	10 Points
Mechanics	5 Points
Neatness	5 Points
	50 Points

Plot Picture

Skill: Differentiate main plot points from details.

What you'll need:

Plot Graphic Organizer (page 32), 9- by 12-inch sheet of construction paper, markers or colored pencils

Steps:

❶ Fill in the Plot Graphic Organizer with the main plot points of the book you have read (see Plotline Guidelines for a description of the plot elements listed on the organizer).

❷ Reread your work and cross out any details that are unnecessary. Only one key event for the introduction, climax, and conclusion and three key events for the rising and falling action sections should remain.

❸ Tape or glue the organizer in the center of the construction paper. On the construction paper, draw at least five simple illustrations that represent the plot points listed on your organizer. Remember to draw each illustration close to the plot event it depicts.

❹ Make sure to include the title and author and your name somewhere on the picture.

Grading Criteria

All main events are described accurately.	20 Points
Pictures reflect the main events of the story.	10 points
Artwork is neat, colorful, and creative.	10 Points
Mechanics	10 Points
	50 Points

Clay Model

Skill: Make symbols with clay to represent the five plot elements from the book you've read.

What you'll need:

Plotline Guidelines (page 31), cardboard or foam board (5 by 12 inches), five fist-sized balls of clay

Steps:

❶ Determine the five plot elements in the book you've read (see Plotline Guidelines for a description of the elements).

❷ Divide your board into five sections and label them: "Introduction," "Rising Action," "Climax," "Falling Action," and "Conclusion."

❸ Create a clay model symbolizing the events that make up each plot element. (For example, you might sculpt a blazing sun or a broken wagon wheel to symbolize the difficulty of a pioneer's journey through a desert.)

❹ Place each clay model in its appropriate space on the board.

❺ On a separate sheet of paper explain how the clay models relate to their corresponding plot elements.

Grading Criteria

There is a clay model for each plot element.	15 Points
Board is labeled correctly.	5 Points
Clay models symbolize important events effectively.	15 Points
Explanation describes symbol and matching plot element.	10 Points
Creativity and neatness	5 Points
	50 Points

Independent Reading Management Kit: Literary Elements   SCHOLASTIC TEACHING RESOURCES

Yearbook

Skill: Identify the main events in a plot sequence and show how they influence future action.

What you'll need:

construction paper, markers or colored pencils

Steps:

❶ Turn the plotline of the book you've read into a typical school year and describe the year with both words and pictures. Each page must have a decorative border to accent the yearbook. Here is what you need for each page:

- Page 1 (Cover): Write the title, author, and a year that relates to the setting of the book.
- Page 2: Title the setting introduction page "School." Draw a picture of the main setting and what it was like there.
- Page 3: Title the character introduction page "Students." Draw pictures of the main and secondary characters with their names listed in captions below as you see in a typical school yearbook.
- Page 4: Title the main-problem page "Beginning of the School Year." Illustrate the main problem that the character faces at the beginning of the book.
- Page 5: Title the rising-action page "As the Year Continues." Draw three significant events that move the plot along toward the climax. Describe the events below the pictures.
- Page 6: Title the climax page "Greatest Memories." Draw the event or events in the story that were the most exciting. Describe them below the picture.
- Page 7: Title the falling-action page "As the Year Winds Down." Draw two to three significant events that happened after the climax. Describe the events below the pictures.
- Page 8: Title the conclusion page "The Last Day of School." Draw a picture of what happens at the end of the book. Describe this event below the drawing.

❷ Feel free to add additional yearbook pages, such as a "Best and Most" page that features the characters who you think have the best looks or personalities, the best problem-solving skills, and so on.

Grading Criteria

Yearbook correctly shows plot events in sequential order.	15 Points
Organization meets criteria set in Step 1.	10 Points
Artwork is neat and colorful.	10 Points
Descriptions explain events thoroughly.	10 Points
Creativity	5 Points
	50 Points

Cube

Plot

Skill: Accurately depict the plotline of a story through art and written expression.

What you'll need:

Cube Template (page 19), Plotline Guidelines (page 31), construction paper, scissors, glue, colored pencils or markers

Steps:

Grading Criteria

Each cube side accurately describes the plot element listed.	15 Points
Sides 2–6 include a simple illustration.	10 Points
All sides of cube include descriptions.	10 Points
Entire cube is neat and colorful.	15 Points
	50 Points

1 Identify the five elements of the plot in the book you've read (see Plotline Guidelines for a description of the elements).

2 Create a six-sided plot cube by following the template. Before you cut it out, write the box title, draw a simple illustration, and write a short caption for each side as follows:
- Side 1: Title and author (no illustration)
- Side 2: Introduction (a scene with the main problem)
- Side 3: Rising action (a scene with the character's attempt to solve the problem)
- Side 4: Climax (a scene representing the highpoint of the story)
- Side 5: Falling action (a scene representing how the problem is finally solved)
- Side 6: Conclusion (the final scene of the book)

3 Cut out, fold along the dotted lines, and glue together the cube, according to the template.

4 Glue the sides of the cube together.

Puppet Show

Plot

Skill: Write and produce a puppet show that recaps the five plot elements.

What you'll need:

markers or colored pencils, glue, socks, paper bags, yarn, and other craft materials, word processor or notebook paper

Steps:

Grading Criteria

Five-act script reflects five plot elements.	15 Points
Script follows book's plot accurately.	15 Points
Mechanics	10 Points
Creative production and use of puppets	10 Points
	50 Points

1 Determine the five elements of the plot in the book you have read (see Plotline Guidelines for a description of each element).

2 Write a script for a five-act play. Each act will illustrate a different plot element.

3 After you've written the script, create puppets and props that will enhance the performance. Remember to create only those things you need to help you explain the main plot elements.

Paper Chain

Skill: Recall and represent the sequence of events in a story in the correct order.

What you'll need:

Plot Graphic Organizer (page 32), sheets of construction paper, glue

Steps:

1 Determine the main plot events of the book you've read and record them on the Plotline Graphic Organizer.

2 Cut 12 strips of construction paper into 2- by 12-inch strips. Using information from the organizer, fill in the strips as follows:

- Strip 1: Title of book and author
- Strip 2: Setting
- Strip 3: A list of the characters
- Strip 4: The main problem
- Strips 5, 6, and 7: Rising-action events
- Strip 8: Climax
- Strips 9, 10, and 11: Falling-action events
- Strip 12: Conclusion

Be sure to label each piece of the chain with the name of the plot element.

3 Glue the chain together with the order of events in proper sequence. Keep the organizer with your chain when you hand in the assignment.

Grading Criteria	
All major events in the plot are included.	20 Points
All events are placed in sequential order.	20 Points
Mechanics	10 Points
	50 Points

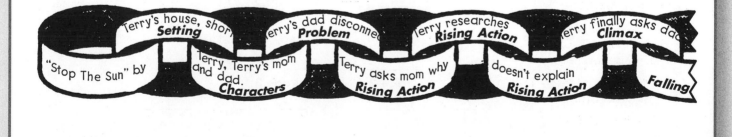

Mini-Picture Book

Skill: Retell the plot of a story in a picture-book format.

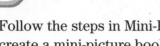

What you'll need:

Mini-Picture Book Directions (Page 33), 8- by 14-inch white legal paper, scissors, markers, crayons or colored pencils, Plotline Guidelines (page 31)

Steps:

❶ Follow the steps in Mini-Picture Book Directions to create a mini-picture book.

❷ Follow these guidelines for each page. Include a written description and a colorful picture that meet the following criteria:

- Page 1: A colorful illustrated cover that includes the title, author, and your name.
- Pages 2 and 3: The introduction (include the setting, main character, and main problem in the story).
- Page 4: Rising-action events
- Page 5: Climax
- Page 6: Falling-action events
- Page 7: Conclusion

Be sure to label the plot elements correctly (see Plotline Guidelines for a description of each element).

Grading Criteria	
Book retells the main parts of the plot.	20 Points
Organization of book follows criteria in Step 2.	10 Points
Descriptions of the plot events are thorough.	10 Points
Artwork is neat, colorful, and reflects written description well.	5 Points
Mechanics	5 Points
	50 Points

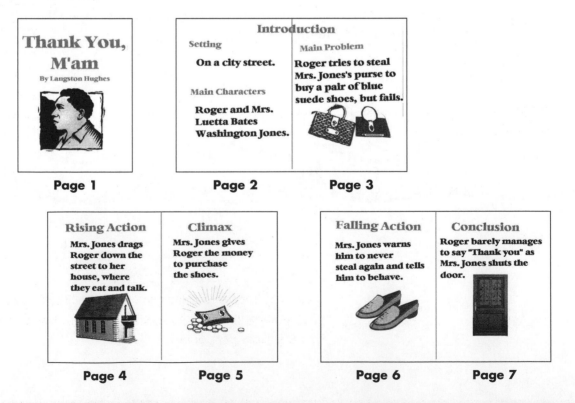

Name: _____ Date: _____

Book Title:_____

PLOTLINE GUIDELINES

These are the five elements you will find in any novel you've read. The formula can help you understand an author's plan.

1. Introduction

- Setting: Where and when the story takes place.
- Characters: Who the story is about. The author's focus is usually on the main character.
- Problem: Conflict in the story and what the characters (usually the main character) have to try to overcome.

2. Rising Action

- Key events that build up to the climax. The character attempts to solve the conflict with different solutions but fails to find a good resolution.

3. Climax

- The high point of the story. Usually it's the most exciting part of the story.

4. Falling Action

- The problem is solved and the loose ends of the story line are being drawn together.

5. Conclusion

- How the story ends.

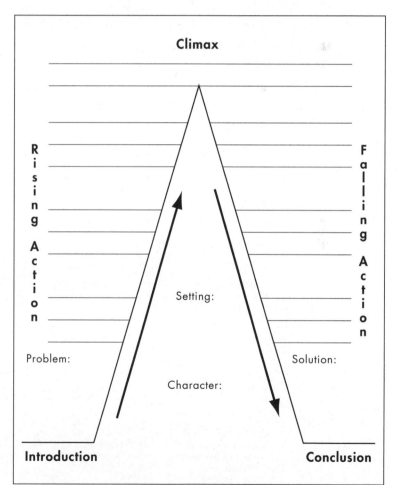

Can you picture the storyline of the whole book? Sometimes it's helpful to map out the plot of a story on a graphic organizer.

Name: _____ Date: _____

PLOT GRAPHIC ORGANIZER

Book title: _____ Author: _____

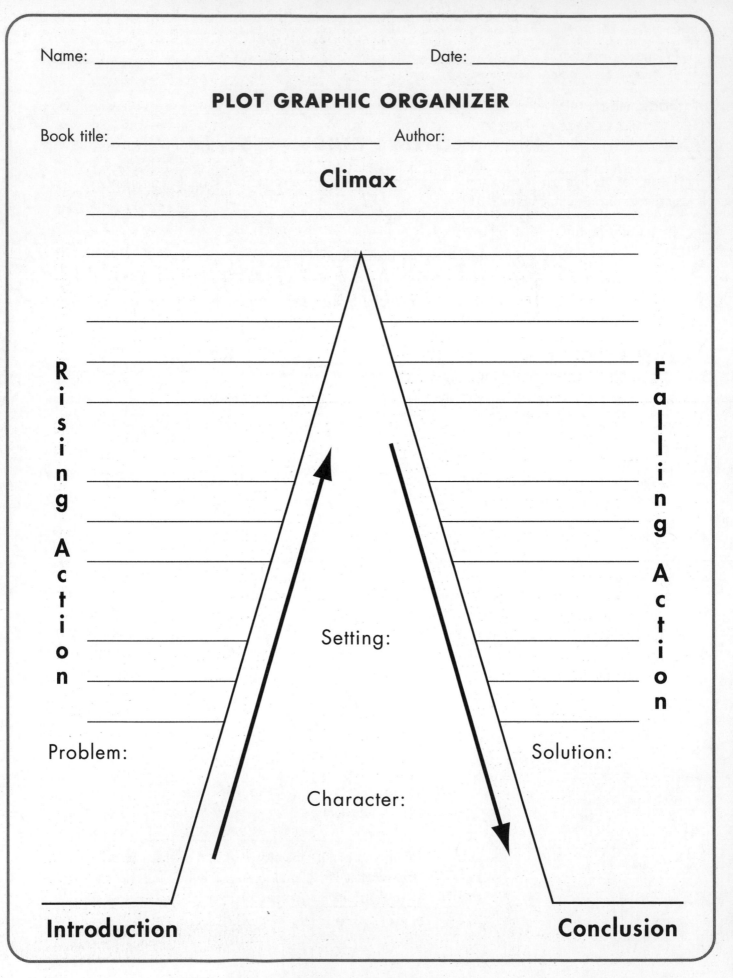

Climax

**R
i
s
i
n
g

A
c
t
i
o
n**

**F
a
l
l
i
n
g

A
c
t
i
o
n**

Setting:

Problem: Solution:

Character:

Introduction   **Conclusion**

Independent Reading Management Kit: Literary Elements   SCHOLASTIC TEACHING RESOURCES

MINI-PICTURE BOOK DIRECTIONS

Use a sheet of construction paper and follow these directions to make an eight-page mini-book.

1. Fold the paper in half, top to bottom. Crease and unfold.

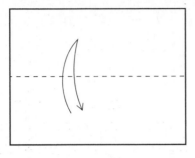

2. Fold the paper in half, left to right. Crease it sharply and leave it folded.

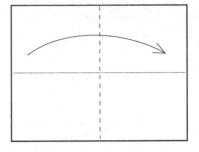

3. Fold again in the same direction. Unfold this last step so that four long boxes face you.

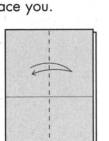

4. Cut a thin line in from the fold between the two middle boxes. Make sure to stop at the middle crease.

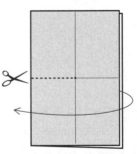

5. Open the whole sheet and fold it in half, top to bottom (lengthwise).

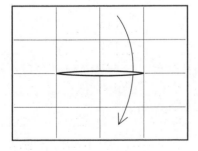

6. Grasp the ends of the sheet and push them together, so that the slit opens and the inner pages of the book are formed.

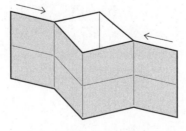

7. Crease the spine of the booklet to form the mini-book. You may have to trim any uneven outside edges so that the mini-book closes properly.

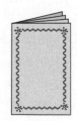

Adapted from *Origami Math: Grades 2–3* © by Karen Baicker, 2004. Published by Scholastic Inc.

Name: _____ Date: _____

GRADING SUMMARY

	Possible Score:	My Score:

☐ **Chart**

Chart accurately represents all five plot elements from the book. — 15 Points _____

Artwork is neat and colorful. — 10 Points _____

Captions describe the pictures well. — 15 Points _____

Mechanics — 5 Points _____

Creativity — 5 Points _____

50 Points _____

☐ **Scrapbook**

Scrapbook accurately displays all plot elements. — 15 Points _____

Scrapbook is creative, colorful, and laid out well. — 15 Points _____

A written explanation of the scrapbook is included on each page. — 10 Points _____

Mechanics — 5 Points _____

Neatness — 5 Points _____

50 Points _____

☐ **Plot Picture**

All main events are described accurately. — 20 Points _____

Pictures reflect the main events of the story. — 10 points _____

Artwork is neat, colorful, and creative. — 10 Points _____

Mechanics — 5 Points _____

Neatness — 5 Points _____

50 Points _____

☐ **Clay Model**

There is an appropriate clay model for each plot element. — 15 Points _____

Board is labeled correctly. — 5 Points _____

Clay models symbolize important events effectively. — 15 Points _____

Explanation describes symbol and matching plot element. — 10 Points _____

Creativity and neatness — 5 Points _____

50 Points _____

Independent Reading Management Kit: Literary Elements SCHOLASTIC TEACHING RESOURCES

☐ Yearbook

Yearbook correctly shows plot events in sequential order.	15 Points	_____
Organization meets criteria set in Step 1.	10 Points	_____
Artwork is neat and colorful.	10 Points	_____
Descriptions explain events thoroughly.	10 Points	_____
Creativity	5 Points	_____
	50 Points	_____

☐ Cube

Each cube side accurately describes the plot element listed.	15 Points	_____
Sides 2–6 include a simple illustration.	10 Points	_____
All sides of cube include descriptions.	10 Points	_____
Entire cube is neat and colorful.	15 Points	_____
	50 Points	_____

☐ Puppet Show

Five-act script reflects five plot elements.	15 Points	_____
Script follows book's plot accurately.	15 Points	_____
Mechanics	10 Points	_____
Creative production and use of puppets	10 Points	_____
	50 Points	_____

☐ Paper Chain

All major events in the plot are included.	20 Points	_____
All events are placed in sequential order.	20 Points	_____
Mechanics	10 Points	_____
	50 Points	_____

☐ Mini-Picture Book

Book retells the main parts of the plot.	20 Points	_____
Organization of book follows criteria in Step 2.	10 Points	_____
Descriptions of the plot events are thorough.	10 Points	_____
Artwork is neat, colorful, and reflects written description well.	5 Points	_____
Mechanics	5 Points	_____
	50 Points	_____

Total for all three projects _____

Character Projects

Name: _____ Due Date: _____

Book Title: _____

Report Card	Memory Box	Character Profile
Trait Flip Book	Who Am I?	Stuffed Character
Character Cards	Shape Analysis	Comparison Poster

Independent Reading Management Kit: Literary Elements   SCHOLASTIC TEACHING RESOURCES

Report Card

Skill: Evaluate a character's strengths across six personality traits.

What you'll need:

Report Card (page 44)

Steps:

Grading Criteria	
Evidence from the reading was used to support grades given.	25 Points
Creativity	15 Points
Mechanics	10 Points
	50 Points

1 Choose a character from the book you've read and grade the character on a scale from A to F for each of the qualities listed on the report card sheet.

2 After you assess the character with letter grades, write comments to describe why the character earned these grades. In other words, give evidence from the story to back up your assessment.

3 In the last box, write a character quality of your choice (for example, intelligent, creative, neat, etc). Then give the character a grade for that quality. Remember to back up your assessment.

Memory Box

Character

Skill: Show how a character developed through the story.

What you'll need:

shoe box, index cards, craft materials

Steps:

Grading Criteria	
Box includes labeled items.	5 Points
Items reflect the character's experiences accurately.	15 Points
Written description explains the item's significance.	15 Points
Creativity	10 Points
Mechanics	5 Points
	50 Points

1 Pick a character from the book you've read. Create a memory box containing seven to nine items that represent significant events in the character's experience during the story.

2 Use a shoe box to store the items and decorate the outside to represent the story. Write a title on the outside: "_name of character_'s Memory Box"

3 Create or collect the items. (Be creative!)

4 Attach an index card to each item that explains the memory that the character associates with the item. Write the memory in first person, as if the character were writing it. For example, if you read _Goldilocks and the Three Bears_ you may include a broken dollhouse chair. Your description may read, "I remember this broken chair because I broke Baby Bear's chair and left the Bear's house a total mess."

Character Profile

Skill: Identify and analyze character traits.

What you'll need:

Picture Sheet (page 45), Birth Certificate (page 46), construction paper, file folder, markers or colored pencils, three to five index cards

Steps:

1 Convince other readers to invite a character you know well into their reading lives. Compile a character profile that gives a true "life" picture of your character. The package you put together must be a factual account of the character based on what you learned from the story. You may need to make a good guess about biographical details that the author does not provide (date of birth, doctor's name).

2 The package you put together must include the following:

    a. A drawing of the character and a written physical description (completed Picture Sheet).

    b. A copy of his or her birth certificate (completed Birth Certificate).

    c. The character's history (choose 3 categories that will help you describe the character, such as family, health, and school). Label each index card with a category and write your description.

    d. A chart listing the character's likes and dislikes.

    e. Anything else you can think of to help others learn more about your character. Be creative!

3 Compile all of these pieces of information and place them in a folder labeled "*Name of Character's* Adoption Package."

Cover

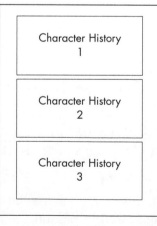

Inside

Trait Flip Book

Skill: Identify a character's personality traits.

What you'll need:

Common Character Traits (page 47), two sheets of 8 1/2- by 11-inch white construction paper, scissors, stapler, markers or colored pencils

Steps:

❶ Choose a character from your reading and pick three traits that the character displayed in the story (use the Common Character Traits for ideas).

❷ Fold two sheets of white construction paper in half lengthwise. Crease them well at the top and put three staples across the top. You now have four pages.

❸ Cut the second, third and fourth pages into thirds about a half inch from the top of your flip book. You now have three equal squares inside the book.

❹ On the cover of the flip book, include the title and author of the book and your own title: "*name of character*'s Trait Flip Book" (e.g., "Miax's Trait Flip Book").

❺ On the second page, write the three traits you chose in the squares.

❻ On the third page, show support for each trait listed on the second page, using examples from the story: Draw a picture of the character displaying these traits and write a caption. For example, you may draw a picture of Miax building a shelter and write, "Miax was brave when she attempted to cross the tundra on her own."

❼ On the last page, draw a picture showing how you also embody this trait and write a caption. For example, you may write "I was brave like Miax when I got stuck in an elevator for three hours and had to keep my little sister calm," and draw a picture of that event.

Grading Criteria

Trait flip book is completed according to directions given.	15 Points
Trait flip book displays three traits that are related to the character.	10 Points
Traits are supported with evidence from the story.	15 Points
Traits are connected to personal experience.	10 Points
	50 Points

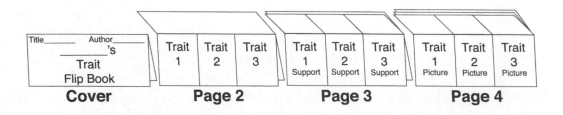

Title_____ Author_____ 's Trait Flip Book	Trait 1	Trait 2	Trait 3	Trait 1 Support	Trait 2 Support	Trait 3 Support	Trait 1 Picture	Trait 2 Picture	Trait 3 Picture
Cover	**Page 2**			**Page 3**			**Page 4**		

Who Am I?

Skill: Use deductive reasoning to write clues about a character's identity.

What you'll need:

ten unlined index cards

Steps:

1 Choose up to ten characters (five minimum) from the book you've read.

2 On the front of each index card write five to seven clues that will help the reader discover the character's identity. Clues can reveal the character's actions, traits, and physical description. Arrange the clues from hardest to easiest so the reader will not guess the identity from the first clue.

3 On the back of the card write the character's name.

Grading Criteria

Clues accurately describe characters' actions, traits, etc.	20 Points
Clues are leveled and arranged well.	15 Points
Mechanics	10 Points
Creativity	5 Points
	50 Points

Stuffed Character

Skill: Analyze a character's thoughts, feelings, and actions.

What you'll need:

Character Symbols (page 48), two sheets of long white bulletin board paper, newspaper to stuff body, creative materials to dress up the body (yarn, pipe cleaners, etc.), scissors, stapler, glue, and markers

Steps:

1 Choose a main character from the book you've read.

2 Lie down lengthwise on a sheet of paper and have a classmate trace an outline of your body with black marker. Cut out the shape, place it on the second sheet, and cut around the outline: Now you have duplicate full-body shapes—one for the back side and another for the front side of your stuffed character.

3 Follow the directions in Character Symbols and complete all parts. Draw each symbol large on the body: thought bubble on the head, speech bubble near the mouth, heart shape in the center of the chest, hand symbol on top of the hands, strength symbol on the arms near the muscles, weakness symbol on the knees. Write the explanation from your Character Symbols page in each symbol and then illustrate the character as you picture him or her.

4 Staple the front and back of the body together, stuffing it with crumpled newspaper as you go. Be careful not to overstuff.

Grading Criteria

Character's appearance is true to the book's description.	15 Points
Symbols accurately represent character's actions, thoughts, feelings.	20 Points
Neatness	5 Points
Mechanics	5 Points
Creativity	5 Points
	50 Points

Character Cards

Skill: Make a character study/sketch.

What you'll need:

five 5- by 8-inch lined index cards, markers or colored pencils

Steps:

1 Create a character card for each of seven to ten characters, using information from the book you've read.

2 Cut each index card in half to make up to ten cards (use a card per character).

3 Set up each character card to resemble a sports collector card. Draw a colorful picture of the character on the front (unlined side). Write his or her name at the bottom and the title of the book at the top. The back (lined side) must include the following:

- The character's "stats": date and place of birth, home town and state, height, weight, and hair and eye color.
- The label "protagonist" or "antagonist," with a short explanation.
- A short phrase or sentence to describe each of the following: character's personality, main action in the story, motivation behind the action (the why), and consequences of the action. The story may not give you all the information you need to complete the card. You may have to infer some of it.

Grading Criteria

Character information is accurate and complete.	15 Points
There are seven to ten cards.	10 Points
Cards meet criteria outlined in Step 3.	15 Points
Creativity	5 Points
Mechanics	5 Points
	50 Points

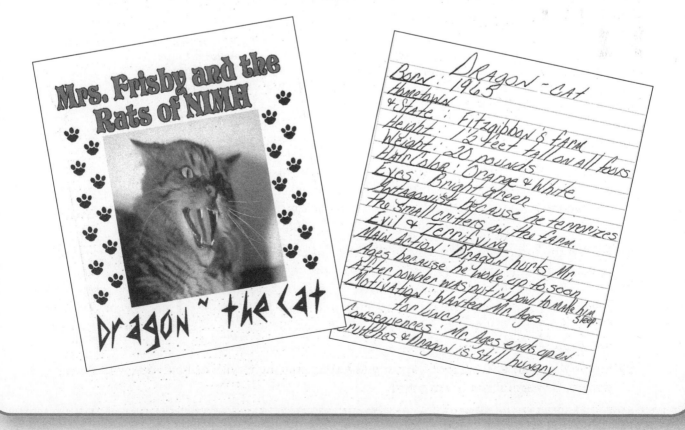

Shape Analysis

Skill: Make associations between shapes and character traits.

What you'll need:

Shape Analysis (page 49), markers or colored pencils

Steps:

❶ Pick four characters you know well from the book you've read.

❷ For three of the characters decide which shape (circle, square, or triangle) best fits each character's personality, actions, and physical characteristics. (Use the attributes of the different shapes to help you: Is the character sharp and angular? Are his or her actions well-rounded or smooth?)

❸ Inside the shape draw a picture of that character. Fill in the lines next to the picture with a description that explains why the character is like that shape.

❹ In the last space, draw any shape that you think matches the character traits of your fourth character and write an explanation.

Grading Criteria	
Shape chosen matches character traits.	15 Points
Explanation shows creative and flexible thinking.	15 Points
Explanation uses support from story.	10 Points
Mechanics	5 Points
Neatness	5 Points
	50 Points

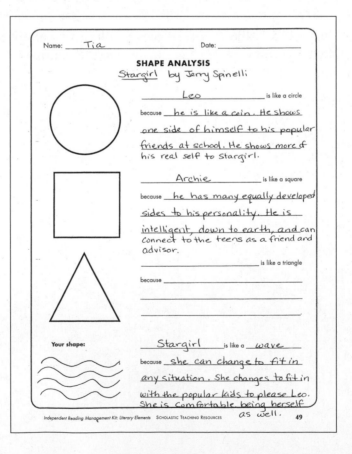

Name: Tia   Date: _____

SHAPE ANALYSIS

Stargirl by Jerry Spinelli

Leo is like a circle because he is like a coin. He shows one side of himself to his popular friends at school. He shows more of his real self to Stargirl.

Archie is like a square because he has many equally developed sides to his personality. He is intelligent, down to earth, and can connect to the teens as a friend and advisor.

_____ is like a triangle because _____

Your shape: Stargirl is like a wave because she can change to fit in any situation. She changes to fit in with the popular kids to please Leo. She is comfortable being herself as well.

Independent Reading Management Kit: Literary Elements SCHOLASTIC TEACHING RESOURCES   49

Comparison Poster

Skill: Compare and contrast a character with yourself.

What you'll need:

a sheet of white construction paper, markers or colored pencils

Steps:

Grading Criteria

Comparison with character is thorough.	20 Points
Poster includes all elements listed in Step 3.	10 Points
Mechanics	10 Points
Neatness and artwork	10 Points
	50 Points

1 Choose a character from the book you've read with whom you feel a connection.

2 Take your construction paper and draw an X through it so it looks like the diagram below.

3 Follow these directions to fill in the page:

- Block 1: Write the title of the book and the author's name. Draw a picture that expresses the main idea of the book.

- Block 2: Label this block "Different." Draw a self-portrait and write your name at the top. List your unique qualities, contrasting them with those of the character you have chosen.

- Block 3: Label this block "Different." Draw a portrait of the character and write his or her name at the top. List the character's unique qualities, contrasting them with your own.

- Block 4: Label this block "Alike." Write a paragraph or two about how you and the character are similar or how you feel connected to the character.

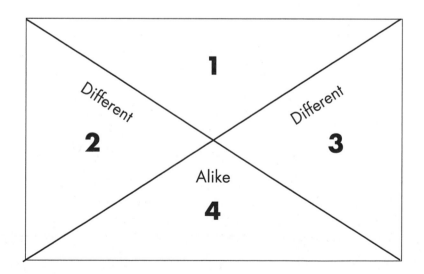

Name: _____ Date: _____

REPORT CARD

Student's (Character's) name

_____

Teacher's (Your) name

_____

Book title

_____

Class Picture

STUDENT QUALITIES	GRADE	COMMENTS
Cooperation/Helpful		
Honesty		
Good Listener		
Responsible		
Imaginative		

Independent Reading Management Kit: Literary Elements SCHOLASTIC TEACHING RESOURCES

Name: _____ Date: _____

PICTURE SHEET

Character name: _____ Age: _____

Height: _____ Weight: _____ Hair color: _____ Eye color: _____

Hobbies: _____

_____

Favorite clothes to wear: _____

_____

Name: _____ Date: _____

Birth Certificate

Gender: Female   Male

Name: _____

Address: _____

Date of birth: _____

Time of birth: _____

Mother's name: _____

Occupation _____

Father's name: _____

Occupation _____

Doctor's name: _____

Registrar's Signature _____

State of _____

Name: _____ Date: _____

COMMON CHARACTER TRAITS

Active	Depressed	Honest	Mischievous	Proud	Tame
Adventurous	Determined	Hostile	Miserly	Prudent	Thankful
Aimless	Disagreeable	Humble	Modest	Questioning	Thoughtful
Ambitious	Distrusted	Immature	Moody	Quick	Timid
Artistic	Dreamer	Impulsive	Mysterious	Quiet	Tireless
Athletic	Dumb	Independent	Nasty	Quirky	Trustworthy
Awesome	Easygoing	Informative	Naughty	Realistic	Thickheaded
Beautiful	Energetic	Intelligent	Neat	Reasonable	Ugly
Belligerent	Entertaining	Inventive	Neglectful	Rebel	Unbiased
Biting	Evil	Jealous	Nice	Reliable	Unethical
Boisterous	Excitable	Jittery	Noble	Remorseful	Unique
Bold	Expert	Joyful	Nosy	Reserved	Unreliable
Bossy	Extravagant	Jovial	Notorious	Respectful	Upstanding
Bouncy	Fancy	Judgmental	Numb	Responsible	Vain
Brave	Fashionable	Kicky	Nutty	Rich	Vicious
Cheerful	Fierce	Kind	Obedient	Rough	Vigilant
Clever	Freakish	Know-it-all	Objective	Rowdy	Villainous
Compassionate	Friendly	Lazy	Observant	Sad	Visionary
Conceited	Fun loving	Lighthearted	Odd	Self-confident	Violent
Considerate	Funny	Loud	Offensive	Selfish	Vibrant
Cooperative	Furious	Lovable	Old-fashioned	Serious	Vocal
Courageous	Generous	Loyal	Open	Sharp	Vulnerable
Creative	Gentle	Lucky	Open-minded	Shy	Warm
Cruel	Gigantic	Malicious	Organized	Silly	Wild
Curious	Graceful	Mature	Patriotic	Simple	Witty
Dainty	Handsome	Mean	Pitiful	Sloppy	Wonderful
Dangerous	Hardworking	Meddling	Plain	Smart	Yielding
Daring	Happy	Melancholy	Poor	Strong	Yucky
Deceptive	Helpful	Mellow	Popular	Studious	Zany
Dedicated	Heroic	Messy	Pretty	Successful	Zealous
Demanding	Hilarious	Merciless	Proper	Tactful	Zestful

Name: _____ Date: _____

CHARACTER SYMBOLS

Character: _____

 Write a quote that best
reveals the character's
personality.

_____
_____

 List words that
describe the character's
feelings.

_____
_____

Describe what the
character thinks about.

_____
_____

Write one strength the
character showed.

_____

Write one weakness
the character showed.

_____

 Explain what the
character attempted to do.

_____
_____
_____
_____

 List the character's
successes and
accomplishments.

_____
_____
_____
_____
_____

Independent Reading Management Kit: Literary Elements   SCHOLASTIC TEACHING RESOURCES

Name: _____ Date: _____

SHAPE ANALYSIS

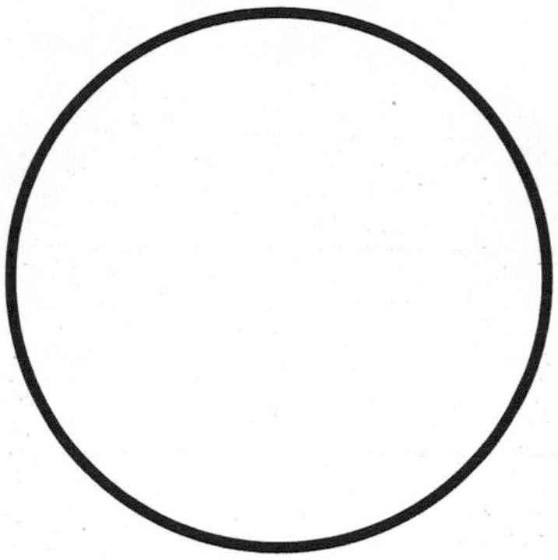

_____ is like a circle

because _____

_____

_____.

_____ is like a square

because _____

_____

_____.

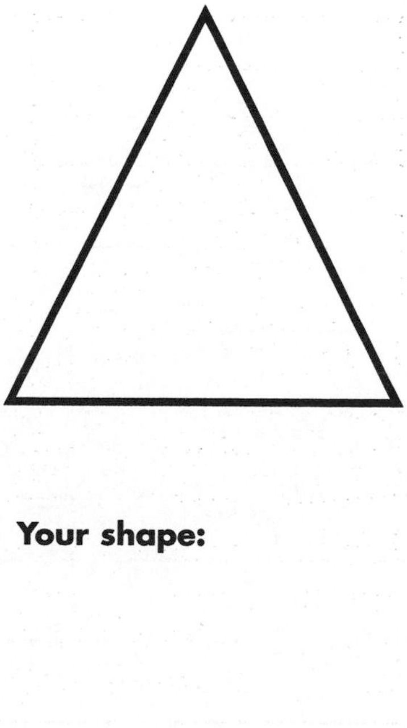

_____ is like a triangle

because _____

_____

_____.

Your shape:

_____ is like a _____

because _____

_____

_____.

Name: _____ Date: _____

GRADING SUMMARY

	Possible Score:	My Score:

☐ **Report Card**

Evidence from the reading was used to support grades given. 25 Points _____

Creativity 15 Points _____

Mechanics 10 Points _____

50 Points _____

☐ **Memory Box**

Box includes labeled items. 5 Points _____

Items reflect the character's experiences accurately. 15 Points _____

Written description explains the item's significance. 15 Points _____

Creativity 10 Points _____

Mechanics 5 Points _____

50 Points _____

☐ **Character Profile**

Package describes character according to facts from the story. 20 Points _____

Parts a–d of the package are included and completed accurately. 15 Points _____

Creativity/extra element (Part e) 10 Points _____

Neatness 5 Points _____

50 Points _____

☐ **Trait Flip Book**

Trait flip book is completed according to directions given. 15 Points _____

Trait flip book displays three traits that are related to the character. 10 Points _____

Traits are supported with evidence from the story. 15 Points _____

Traits are connected to personal experience. 10 Points _____

50 Points _____

□ **Who Am I?**

Clues accurately describe characters' actions, traits, etc.	20 Points _____
Clues are leveled and arranged well.	15 Points _____
Mechanics	10 Points _____
Creativity	5 Points _____
	50 Points _____

□ **Stuffed Character**

Character's appearance is true to the book's description.	15 Points _____
Symbols accurately represent character's actions, thoughts, feelings.	20 Points _____
Neatness	5 Points _____
Mechanics	5 Points _____
Creativity	5 Points _____
	50 Points _____

□ **Character Cards**

Character information is accurate and complete.	15 Points _____
There are seven to ten cards.	10 Points _____
Cards meet criteria outlined in Step 3.	15 Points _____
Creativity	5 Points _____
Mechanics	5 Points _____
	50 Points _____

□ **Shape Analysis**

Shape chosen matches character traits.	15 Points _____
Explanation shows creative and flexible thinking.	15 Points _____
Explanation uses support from story.	10 Points _____
Mechanics	5 Points _____
Neatness	5 Points _____
	50 Points _____

□ **Comparison Poster**

Comparison with character is thorough.	20 Points _____
Poster includes all elements listed in Step 3.	10 Points _____
Mechanics	10 Points _____
Neatness and artwork	10 Points _____
	50 Points _____

Total for all three projects _____

Point of View and Character Perspective Projects

Name: _____ Due Date: _____

Book Title: _____

Readers Theater	**Rewrite**	**Fractured Version**
Newspaper	**Quotes Quiz**	**Inanimate Object**
Advertisement Poster	**Want/Need Poster**	**Quotation Cootie Catcher**

Independent Reading Management Kit: Literary Elements SCHOLASTIC TEACHING RESOURCES

Readers Theater

Skill: Reformulate narrative text into script form.

What you'll need:

pen and paper or a word processor

Steps:

1 Choose any chapter from the book you've read and rewrite it in script form so that it may be performed as a play by a Readers Theater group.

2 Your script must include the following:

- the title of the book, author's name, and title of the chapter from which you adapted the scene (write these at the top of the first page)
- a list of the characters involved in the play
- a narrator, to set the stage and reveal what has happened in previous chapters
- stage directions (character actions, facial expressions, sound effects, and so on) written in parentheses, so the actors know where to go and what to do

3 Ask a few classmates to help you perform your play for the class.

Grading Criteria	
Chapter is written in script form.	15 Points
Script meets criteria in Step 2.	20 Points
Creativity with stage directions, expressions, etc.	10 Points
Mechanics	5 Points
	50 Points

Rewrite

Skill: Rewrite a part of the story from another point of view and analyze how the changes affect the text.

What you'll need:

pen and paper or word processor

Steps:

1 Choose a chapter from the book you've read and rewrite it from another point of view. For example, if the story was told from a third-person point of view, you might want to write it in first person or from another character's point of view.

2 When you finish, double-check that you have written the entire chapter from this new point of view.

3 On the back of your rewrite, discuss which point of view worked better and why. (Is it better to hear the voice of a character who is close to the action of the story or a character who is more removed?)

Grading Criteria	
Rewrite consistently represents another point of view.	20 Points
Rewrite retells all events in the chapter effectively.	20 Points
Mechanics	5 Points
Creativity	5 Points
	50 Points

Fractured Version

Skill: Reformulate the text by changing one or several aspects.

Point of View

What you'll need:

Storyboard (page 60), pen and paper or word processor

Steps:

❶ Imagine you are a children's book author and your publisher has asked you to write and illustrate a "fractured" version of the book you've read. In a fractured version of a book, certain aspects of the story, such as the setting, characters, problem, and point of view are changed. Your publisher wants you to change *at least* the point of view in the story. (One famous fractured version, *The True Story of the Three Little Pigs* by Jon Scieszka, retells the original story from the wolf's point of view. Seek out this book if you need help fracturing your story.)

❷ Use the storyboard as a rough draft to help you organize your story. There are twelve squares, and each completed square, called a "thumbnail," represents a page of your book. The first square represents your book's cover. In this square write the title of your fractured story and your name. Fill in the remaining eleven squares with notes and sketches for the full plot of the book. Make sure that when you are organizing your story, it still has a beginning, middle, and end.

❸ Using your thumbnail sketches from your storyboard, create an eleven-page children's book. Include illustrations that fill up each page and story text to match the picture. Pictures may be hand drawn or computer generated.

Newspaper

Skill: Write a newspaper article from an objective point of view.

What you'll need:

5 W's Organizer (page 61), Newspaper Template (page 62), markers or colored pencils

Steps:

❶ Imagine that you are a newspaper reporter who has been asked to interview and write a feature article about the main character in the book you've read. Write the article from your point of view as an objective reporter who just reports the facts.

❷ First come up with ten or more interview questions that will encourage the main character to give you lots of detailed, personal information. Write the interview questions on the organizer and fill in the answers as the character would.

❸ Use the answers from your interview to create a newspaper front page. Use the template to help you organize your thoughts.

❹ Give your newspaper a title, a catchy headline, a lead story with at least two quotes from the main character, two story-related pictures with captions, and an advertisement that would appeal to fellow readers of the book.

❺ The newspaper may be hand drawn or computer generated or a combination of both.

Grading Criteria

Ten or more well-written interview questions and character-appropriate responses	15 Points
Newspaper is organized according to criteria in Step 4 and template.	15 Points
Lead article is written from an objective point of view.	15 Points
Mechanics	5 Points
	50 Points

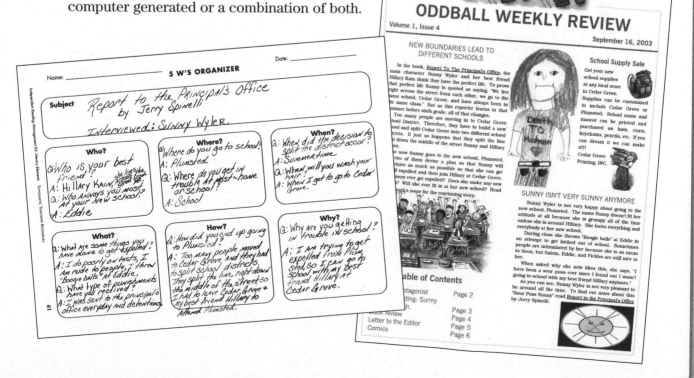

Quotes Quiz

Character Perspective

Skill: Identify key character voices and show how specific quotations affect the story line.

What you'll need:

15 to 20 index cards

Steps:

1 Pick 15 to 20 quotes from different characters in the book you've read.

2 On the front of each index card, copy a quote exactly as it appears in the story. On the back, write the name of the character who said those words and explain why the quotation was important to the story line. (Did it show a change in the way a character behaves? foreshadow another event? change another character's opinion and resulting actions?)

3 You may use a character no more than three times during your quiz.

4 Present your quiz to the class by reading the quote and letting the class guess who said it. Give extra points if the player can explain why the quotation was important to the story.

Grading Criteria

Quotes are correctly matched to characters.	25 Points
Quotes are important to the story line.	15 Points
Neatness	10 Points
	50 Points

Inanimate Object

Point of View

Skill: Rewrite a scene from the point of view of an inanimate object that was in the story.

What you'll need:

pen and paper or word processor

Steps:

1 Imagine that you have been sucked into the book you've read and you have become an inanimate object from the story. Retell a scene or chapter from the point of view of that object. (For example, from the story *Jack and the Beanstalk* you might chose to write from the point of view of the beanstalk, the golden harp, or the golden eggs.)

2 In a one- or two-page retelling you must reveal what you are, describe how it feels to be that thing, and relate the details of the events of the scene or chapter from your point of view. Make sure to use descriptive language that appeals to the senses.

Grading Criteria

Scene/chapter is accurately and appropriately told from the object's point of view.	15 Points
Language used is descriptive.	10 Points
Retelling is complete.	10 Points
Creativity	10 Points
Mechanics	5 Points
	50 Points

Advertisement Poster

Skill: Create an advertisement that appeals to one character's perspective.

Character Perspective

What you'll need:

8 1/2- by 11-inch white construction paper, markers or colored pencils

Steps:

❶ Develop a new product and create an advertisement poster for it that would appeal to a character from the book you've read. (For example, you might create a poster advertising sturdy, no-crumble bricks for the third little pig from the story *The Three Little Pigs* because he needed high-quality bricks to build his wolf-proof house.)

❷ Your advertisement poster must include the following:
- a colorful picture of the item you are advertising
- a catchy slogan or headline
- a paragraph describing the product (use all 5 senses)
- where to buy it, whom to contact for more information, and the cost involved

❸ On the back of your poster, provide a short write-up that identifies the character to whom you are appealing and explains why that character would be interested in this product.

Grading Criteria	
Poster is created to persuade character to purchase product.	10 Points
Description of product is detailed.	10 Points
Write-up explains why it appeals to that particular character.	15 Points
Layout of poster is neat, appealing, and colorful.	10 Points
Mechanics	5 Points
	50 Points

The stain-free trouser ad would appeal to 6-year-old Little Man from "Roll of Thunder, Hear My Cry." He would be interested in this ad because he is obsessed with keeping his clothes spotless at all times.

INTRODUCING THE NEW STAIN-FREE TROUSER THAT WILL RESIST ANY KIND OF STAIN. THESE TROUSERS WILL STAY CLEAN EVEN WHEN THE JEFFERSON DAVIS SCHOOL BUS ZOOMS DOWN THE ROAD AND SLINGS MUD AND MUCK AT YOU.
PURCHASE YOURS TODAY IN ANY MERCANTILE IN STRAWBERRY. COST IS NEGOTIABLE AND A TRADE CAN BE WORKED OUT.

Want/Need Poster

Skill: Identify wants and needs from one character's perspective.

Character Perspective

What you'll need:

8 1/2- by 11-inch white construction paper, Internet access, and markers or colored pencils

Steps:

1 Identify something that a character from the book you've read wants or needs.

2 Design your poster as an Old West "wanted" poster created by that character. (Conduct a general search on the Internet and type "wanted posters" to see some samples and get design ideas.)

3 Write the title "Wanted" or "Needed" at the top and then "By _character's name_" as the attention getter. In the middle, draw a big picture that shows the want or need. The bottom portion of your poster must include these "vital statistics":

- the name of the object the character wants or needs
- a detailed description of the object (use all 5 senses)
- why the character wants/needs the object

Grading Criteria	
Want/Need Poster is appropriate for chosen character.	15 Points
Vital statistics are accurate.	10 Points
Directions for the project were followed.	10 Points
Layout of poster is neat, organized, and colorful.	10 Points
Mechanics	5 Points
	50 Points

WANTED
By Nick Allen

A Frindle

Vital Statistics:

Nick Allen from the book "Frindle" wants everyone including his teacher, Mrs. Granger, to start calling a pen a frindle. A frindle is a long, thin instrument for writing that comes in a variety of styles and colors. A frindle can be found in any type of store, in a woman's purse, under couch cushions, or in a school. Nick Allen wants everyone to call a pen a frindle to prove to his dictionary-loving fifth grade teacher that he is right and she is wrong. If anyone has seen a frindle please contact Nick Allen at once at ✱✱✱-nopen.

Quotation Cootie Catcher

Skill: Use character quotes from the story to create an interactive game.

What you'll need:

How to Make a Cootie Catcher direction sheet (page 63), a sheet of white copy paper, markers or colored pencils

Steps:

1 Pick a hot topic from the book you've read—a topic about which many characters feel differently. Find or write eight quotations that show the perspectives of several characters on this topic. You may use a character no more than twice.

2 After choosing your eight quotes, make a cootie catcher, using the directions sheet. On one side of the cootie catcher will be four squares. On the first square write the title of the book; on the second square, the author; on the third square, your name; and on the fourth square draw a picture to represent the book.

3 Turn over your cootie catcher and number the triangles 1 to 8. Write a quote on each triangle, open the triangle, and under the flap write the name of the character who said it. Make sure quotes from the book are copied exactly and appear with quotation marks.

4 Present the finished game to the class. Ask other students for a number. Read the quote that's written on the matching flap and let them guess from which character's perspective that quote is written.

Grading Criteria

Cootie catcher is set up according to criteria in Steps 2 and 3.	20 Points
Quotes are correctly matched to characters.	20 Points
Neatness	5 Points
Mechanics	5 Points
	50 Points

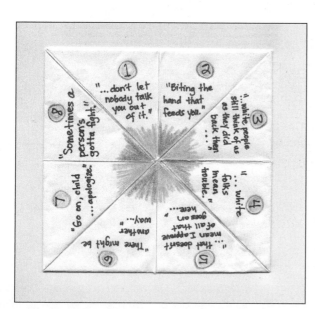

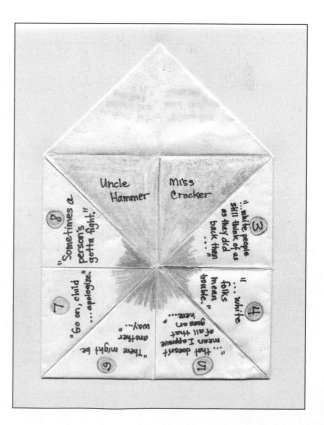

Name: _____ Date: _____

STORYBOARD

1	**2**	**3**
4	**5**	**6**
7	**8**	**9**
10	**11**	**12**

Independent Reading Management Kit: Literary Elements   SCHOLASTIC TEACHING RESOURCES

Name: _____

Date: _____

5 W'S ORGANIZER

Subject

Who?

Where?

When?

What?

How?

Why?

Name: _____ Date: _____

_____
title of newspaper

Vol. 1   **Date:** _____

headline

news story

caption

news story

advertisement

caption

Name: _____ Date: _____

HOW TO MAKE A COOTIE CATCHER

1. Cut a square piece of paper. Fold the square in half to make a triangle.

2. Unfold the paper to show a square and fold it the other way to make a new triangle.

3. Unfold the paper to show a square again.

4. Fold each corner to the center.

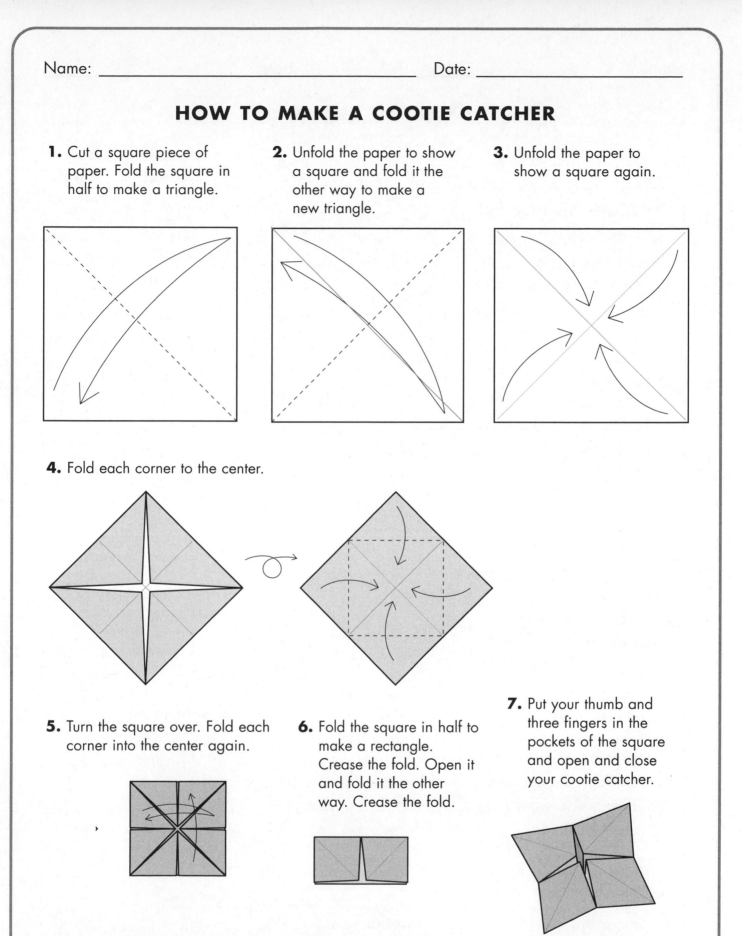

5. Turn the square over. Fold each corner into the center again.

6. Fold the square in half to make a rectangle. Crease the fold. Open it and fold it the other way. Crease the fold.

7. Put your thumb and three fingers in the pockets of the square and open and close your cootie catcher.

Adapted from *Origami Math: Grades 4–6* © by Karen Baicker, 2004. Published by Scholastic Inc.

Name: _____ Date: _____

GRADING SUMMARY

	Possible Score:	My Score:

☐ **Readers Theater**

	Possible Score:	My Score:
Chapter is written in script form.	15 Points	_____
Script meets criteria in Step 2.	20 Points	_____
Creativity with stage directions, expressions, etc.	10 Points	_____
Mechanics	5 Points	_____
	50 Points	_____

☐ **Rewrite**

	Possible Score:	My Score:
Rewrite consistently represents another point of view.	20 Points	_____
Rewrite retells all events in the chapter effectively.	20 Points	_____
Mechanics	5 Points	_____
Creativity	5 Points	_____
	50 Points	_____

☐ **Fractured Version**

	Possible Score:	My Score:
Picture book creatively fractures original story.	15 Points	_____
Story still has a beginning, middle, and end.	15 Points	_____
Illustrations match text.	10 Points	_____
Book is neat and colorful.	10 Points	_____
	50 Points	_____

☐ **Newspaper**

	Possible Score:	My Score:
Ten or more well-written interview questions and character-appropriate responses	15 Points	_____
Newspaper is organized according to criteria in Step 4 and template.	15 Points	_____
Lead article is written from an objective point of view.	15 Points	_____
Mechanics	5 Points	_____
	50 Points	_____

□ **Quotes Quiz**

Quotes are correctly matched to characters.   25 Points _____

Quotes are important to the story line.   15 Points _____

Neatness   10 Points _____

                                                                        50 Points _____

□ **Inanimate Object**

Scene/chapter is accurately and appropriately told from the
object's point of view.   15 Points _____

Language used is descriptive.   10 Points _____

Retelling is complete.   10 Points _____

Creativity   10 Points _____

Mechanics   5 Points _____

                                                                        50 Points _____

□ **Advertisement Poster**

Poster is created to persuade character to purchase product.   10 Points _____

Description of product is detailed.   10 Points _____

Write-up explains why it appeals to that particular character.   15 Points _____

Layout of poster is neat, appealing, and colorful.   10 Points _____

Mechanics   5 Points _____

                                                                        50 Points _____

□ **Want/Need Poster**

Want/Need Poster is appropriate for chosen character.   15 Points _____

Vital statistics are accurate.   10 Points _____

Directions for the project were followed.   10 Points _____

Layout of poster is neat, organized, and colorful.   10 Points _____

Mechanics   5 Points _____

                                                                        50 Points _____

□ **Quotation Cootie Catcher**

Cootie catcher is set up according to criteria in Steps 2 and 3.   20 Points _____

Quotes are correctly matched to characters.   20 Points _____

Neatness   5 Points _____

Mechanics   5 Points _____

                                                                        50 Points _____

Total for all three projects _____

Theme Projects

Name: _____ Due Date: _____

Book Title: _____

CD Cover	Organizer	Diamante
Puzzle	Progression Chart	Theme Song
Banner	Promotional Products	ABC Book

CD Cover

Skill: Represent the story's theme in a musical album design.

What you'll need:

clear, empty CD cover (jewel case), a sheet of white copy paper, scissors, markers or colored pencils

Grading Criteria

Songs and cover image connect to the theme(s) of the book.	15 Points
Explanations clearly show connections to the theme(s).	15 Points
CD cover is designed according to criteria in Step 2.	10 Points
Creativity	5 Points
Neatness	5 Points
	50 Points

Steps:

1 Imagine that you have signed a deal with a big record company to create a soundtrack for the book you've read. Brainstorm ideas for a CD album cover that will show a memorable image and a back cover that lists song titles. The whole album must communicate the theme or themes of the book.

2 Cut your sheet of paper into two squares that fit into the clear CD cover. Staple or tape them together along one side to create a booklet. Then design it to include the following:

- a front cover with the title of the book, the author, and a colorful illustration that shows the main theme of the story.

- a back cover that lists seven to ten song titles by artists whose work you feel matches the theme(s) of the book. For example, if you are reading *Holes* by Louis Sachar, a song title might be "Eye of the Tiger" by Survivor because it speaks to the theme of courage. The main character, Stanley, shows courage when he steals the truck, carries Zero up the mountain, and sticks up for himself in the "wreck" room.

- an interior page or pages that explains why you chose each song and how it relates to the theme of the book. (Use the back of the cover and back cover sheets.)

Organizer

Skill: Identify the story's theme and use evidence from the text for support.

What you'll need:

Theme Organizer template (page 73), a sheet of white copy paper, markers or colored pencils

Steps:

1 Using the template, determine the big idea of the book you've read. Fill in the middle box with supporting evidence from the story—what the characters say and do. Fill in the bottom box with "what is important to learn," or the theme of the story.

2 Using the template as a rough draft, recopy the organizer onto a clean sheet of paper. This time turn the boxes into shapes or objects from the story to match the theme. For example, chains and a dress can represent a character's dependence on material possessions.

Grading Criteria

Big idea and the theme of the story are correctly identified. 15 Points

Organizer shows evidence from the story to support theme. 15 Points

Final copy graphics relate to the story's theme. 15 Points

Creativity 5 Points

50 Points

Diamante

Skill: Describe the story's theme in a diamante poem format.

What you'll need:

Diamante Poetry (page 74), Common Themes in Literature (page 75), scissors, construction paper, markers or colored pencils

Steps:

1 Follow the directions given in Diamante Poetry. Make sure that Line 1 of your poem communicates the main theme of the book you've read and that the rest of the poem supports the theme.

2 Cut out your poem and create a background design that relates to the story's theme in some way. For example, if the story's theme was "Love your neighbor," you can paste your poem on a big heart.

3 If you are having trouble determining the theme of your story, refer to Common Themes in Literature.

Grading Criteria

Theme of the story is correctly identified. 15 Points

Diamante poem follows guidelines. 15 Points

Background design supports theme of the story. 10 Points

Neatness 5 Points

Mechanics 5 Points

50 Points

Puzzle

Skill: Identify the author's message and show evidence from the story.

What you'll need:

Puzzle Pieces (page 76), markers or colored pencils, laminator to laminate puzzle pieces (optional)

Grading Criteria

Themes from the story are correctly identified.	20 Points
Evidence from the story is used to support themes.	20 Points
Puzzles pieces fit together well.	5 Points
Neatness	5 Points
	50 Points

Steps:

1 Identify three main messages (themes) the author of the book you've read is trying to communicate. Find evidence from the story to back up your choices.

2 For each puzzle-piece set on Puzzle Pieces, write a theme on one of the puzzle pieces. Fill in the other three pieces of the set with evidence from the story to support the theme. Do the same with the other puzzle-piece sets. Feel free to create your own puzzle patterns if you would like.

3 Cut out your puzzle pieces and have a classmate try to piece your theme-evidence puzzles together. (Your teacher may be able to laminate the puzzles for durability.)

Progression Chart

Skill: Chart the progression of the story's theme.

What you'll need:

Theme Progression Chart (page 77), markers or colored pencils

Grading Criteria

Theme is explained for each stage of the story.	15 Points
Supporting evidence from the book is used.	15 Points
Pictures match the themes.	15 Points
Mechanics	5 Points
	50 Points

Steps:

1 As you are reading or reviewing the story, think about the author's main message.

2 Record what you think the message is in the beginning, middle, and end on the chart. For each part of the story, write a sentence or two describing what you think the theme may be. Use evidence from the story to support your idea. Draw pictures in the boxes to match your theme ideas.

Theme Song

Skill: Restate the story's theme in song lyrics.

What you'll need:

notebook paper

Steps:

❶ Imagine that you are a songwriter and you have found out that the book you've read will be turned into a new TV show. You have been assigned by the show's producer to create the theme song for this new show.

❷ Identify the overall theme of the story and create a song that will run before the show begins. The theme song should last about 30 seconds. (Think about the theme songs of current TV shows for inspiration. Feel free to use a common rhyme and change the lyrics.)

❸ Explain the meaning of the song and how it relates to the theme in a short paragraph on the back of the lyrics.

❹ Perform the song for your classmates.

Grading Criteria

Song accurately reflects the theme of the story.	20 Points
Explanation shows how song relates to the theme.	15 Points
Creativity	10 Points
Mechanics	5 Points
	50 Points

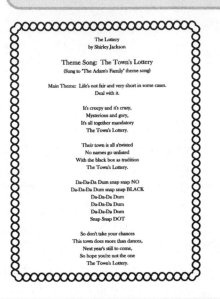

The Lottery
by Shirley Jackson

Theme Song: The Town's Lottery
(Sung to "The Adam's Family" theme song)

Main Theme: Life's not fair and very short in some cases.
Deal with it.

It's creepy and it's crazy,
Mysterious and gory,
It's all together mandatory
The Town's Lottery.

Their town is all a'twisted
No names go unlisted
With the black box as tradition
The Town's Lottery.

Da-Da-Da Dum snap snap NO
Da-Da-Da Dum snap snap BLACK
Da-Da-Da Dum
Da-Da-Da Dum
Da-Da-Da Dum
Snap Snap DOT

So don't take your chances
This town does more than dances,
Next year's still to come,
So hope you're not the one
The Town's Lottery.

Banner

Skill: Restate the story's theme visually.

What you'll need:

posterboard, magazines, newspapers, computer clip art, glue, and markers

Steps:

❶ To create a banner (any shape you wish) that represents the theme of the book you've read, gather or draw illustrations (from magazines, newspapers, clip art, or your own sketchbook). These images must be related to the story and depict the theme.

❷ In the center of your banner write the book's title and author.

❸ On the back of your banner, write a short paragraph explaining the significance of the pictures you've used and how they relate to the story's theme.

Grading Criteria

Banner effectively illustrates/represents the theme of the book.	15 points
Banner's layout is pleasing to look at.	10 Points
Paragraph explains the significance of the pictures on the banner and how they relate to the theme.	15 Points
Neatness	10 Points
	50 Points

Promotional Products

Skill: Represent the theme of a book as a marketable product.

Theme

What you'll need:

scrap paper for sketching, construction paper, scissors, glue, markers, crayons, colored pencils, various creative supplies such as glitter, yarn, etc.

Steps:

❶ Imagine that you are a marketing executive who has been asked to create four promotional products to sell along with the book you've read.

❷ First, come up with a logo that best represents the theme of the book and will promote sales of the book. (Consider company logos that stick with you, such as a symbol for a video game or fast food restaurant.)

❸ Sketch four product ideas that support the theme (T-shirts, key chains, magnets, mugs, hats, snow globes, etc.). Be creative!

❹ Draw a final picture of the products on the construction paper. Make sure to include on each product the book title, the author's name, and the logo that you designed.

❺ Prepare a short write-up that explains how the logo you created and each product supports the theme.

Grading Criteria

Logo represents the theme.	15 Points
The four products are appropriate to the theme.	10 points
Write-up explains how the logo and products are connected to the theme.	15 Points
Creativity	10 points
	50 Points

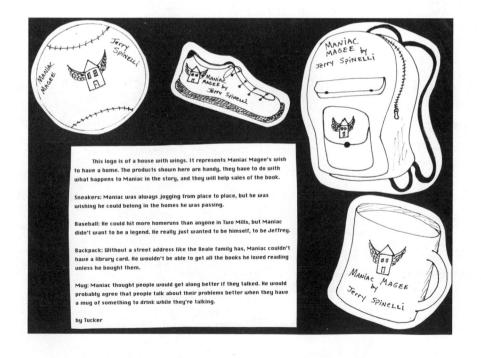

ABC Book

Skill: Synthesize the themes of a book in an ABC book format.

What you'll need:

ABC Book Planner (page 78), white copy paper, computer word processing program with clip art, markers or colored pencils, materials to bind the book (brads, yarn, string, or binder)

Steps:

1 Use the ABC Book Planner chart to plan the layout for an ABC book based on the book you've read. For each letter on the chart, write a word or phrase that begins with the letter and supports a theme from the book. Think of a word or phrase to match each letter of the alphabet that relates to the theme.

2 For each ABC book page, type or write the word or phrase you brainstormed for the featured alphabet letter, draw or design a picture that represents it, and type or write an explanation of how the text and picture support the theme of the book. You may be able to fit two or three letters per page.

3 Bind the pages of your ABC book together.

Grading Criteria	
Each letter of the alphabet has a word or phrase that relates to the theme of the book.	15 points
Each letter has a picture to match and an explanation of how it supports the theme.	20 Points
All letters of the alphabet are represented.	5 Points
Creativity	5 Points
Mechanics	5 Points
	50 Points

Name: _____   Date: _____

THEME ORGANIZER

Big Idea or Topic

What Characters Say or Do

Important Lesson Learned (Theme)

DIAMANTE POETRY

A diamante poem is a seven-line poem that is shaped like a diamond.

Line 1: One word to represent the theme (must contrast with Line 7)

Line 2: Two adjectives that describe or support Line 1

Line 3: Three verbs that relate to Line 1

Line 4: Four nouns (the first two relate to Line 1, the next two relate to Line 7)

Line 5: Three verbs that relate to Line 7

Line 6: Two adjectives that describe or support Line 7

Line 7: One word that contrasts with Line 1

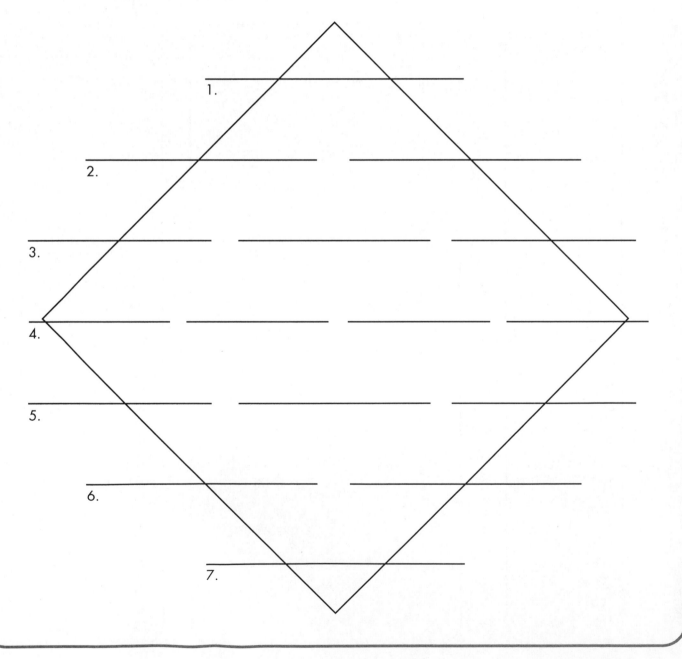

COMMON THEMES IN LITERATURE

- childhood
- courage
- death
- faith
- family
- freedom
- friendship
- greed
- growing up
- hate
- hope
- identity
- independence
- jealousy
- justice
- love

- loyalty
- nature
- patience
- patriotism
- prejudice
- pride
- race relations
- self-improvement
- self-reliance
- success
- survival
- trust
- truth
- unhappiness
- violence
- war

Name: _____ Date: _____

PUZZLE PIECES

Independent Reading Management Kit: Literary Elements   Scholastic Teaching Resources

Name: _____ Date: _____

THEME PROGRESSION CHART

Beginning

_____
_____
_____
_____
_____
_____

Middle

_____
_____
_____
_____
_____
_____

End

_____
_____
_____
_____
_____
_____

Name: _____ Date: _____

ABC BOOK PLANNER

A	B	C	D
E	F	G	H
I	J	K	L
M	N	O	P
Q	R	S	T
U	V	W	X
	Y	Z	

Independent Reading Management Kit: Literary Elements   SCHOLASTIC TEACHING RESOURCES

Name: _____ Date: _____

GRADING SUMMARY

	Possible Score:	My Score:

☐ **CD Cover**

Songs and cover image connect to the theme(s) of the book. 15 Points _____

Explanations clearly show connections to the theme(s). 15 Points _____

CD cover is designed according to criteria in Step 2. 10 Points _____

Creativity 5 Points _____

Neatness 5 Points _____

50 Points _____

☐ **Organizer**

Big idea and the theme of the story are correctly identified. 15 Points _____

Organizer shows evidence from the story to support theme. 15 Points _____

Final copy graphics relate to the story's theme. 15 Points _____

Creativity 5 Points _____

50 Points _____

☐ **Diamante**

Theme of the story is correctly identified. 15 Points _____

Diamante poem follows guidelines. 15 Points _____

Background design supports theme of the story. 10 Points _____

Neatness 5 Points _____

Mechanics 5 Points _____

50 Points _____

☐ **Puzzle**

Themes from the story are correctly identified. 20 Points _____

Evidence from the story is used to support themes. 20 Points _____

Puzzles pieces fit together well. 5 Points _____

Neatness 5 Points _____

50 Points _____

☐ **Progression Chart**

Theme is explained for each stage of the story.	15 Points	_____
Supporting evidence from the book is used.	15 Points	_____
Pictures match the themes.	15 Points	_____
Mechanics	5 Points	_____
	50 Points	_____

☐ **Theme Song**

Song accurately reflects the theme of the story.	20 Points	_____
Explanation shows how song relates to the theme.	15 Points	_____
Creativity	10 Points	_____
Mechanics	5 Points	_____
	50 Points	_____

☐ **Banner**

Banner effectively illustrates/represents the theme of the book.	15 points	_____
Banner's layout is pleasing to look at.	10 Points	_____
Paragraph explains the significance of the pictures on the banner and how they relate to the theme.	15 Points	_____
Neatness	10 Points	_____
	50 Points	_____

☐ **Promotional Products**

Logo represents the theme.	15 Points	_____
The four products are appropriate to the theme.	10 points	_____
Write-up explains how the logo and products are connected to the theme.	15 Points	_____
Creativity	10 points	_____
	50 Points	_____

☐ **ABC Book**

Each letter of the alphabet has a word or phrase that relates to the theme of the book.	15 points	_____
Each letter has a picture to match and an explanation of how it supports the theme.	20 Points	_____
All letters of the alphabet are represented.	5 Points	_____
Creativity	5 Points	_____
Mechanics	5 Points	_____
	50 Points	_____

Total for all three projects _____

Conflict Projects

Name: _____ Due Date: _____

Book Title: _____

Sandwich Board	**Silhouette**	**Pictorial Representation**
Evaluation Grid	**Acrostic Poem**	**Question Mark**
Bookmark	**Analyze This!**	**Prove It!**

Sandwich Board

Skill: Describe a person-versus-person conflict from the perspectives of two characters.

Conflict

What you'll need:

two sheets of posterboard, hole puncher, string or yarn, and markers

Steps:

❶ A sandwich board is a walking advertisement made of two connected signs that hang from a person's shoulders, a sign in front and the other on the back. Choose a conflict between two characters in the book you've read and create a sandwich board that shows the conflict from each perspective.

❷ At the top of both boards, write the book's title and name of the author.

❸ On the first board, illustrate the conflict and describe it in complete detail from one character's point of view. Label it "_name of character_'s Side."

❹ Repeat Step 3 on the second board to show the other character's point of view.

❺ Punch two holes at the top of each posterboard and attach them with string or yarn. Put the sandwich board on and present the conflict to the class.

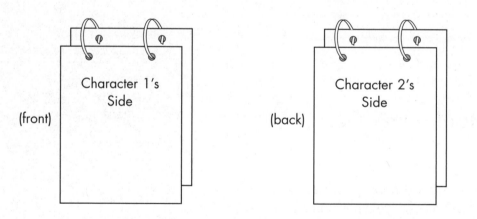

Character 1's Side (front)   Character 2's Side (back)

Silhouette

Conflict

Skill: Describe a person-versus-self conflict.

What you'll need:

white construction paper, thick black marker

Steps:

1 In a person-versus-self conflict, a character struggles with his or her own emotions, conscience, or physical abilities. Pick a character from the book you've read who exhibits such a conflict.

2 On white construction paper make a large silhouette (a drawing of the character's profile— a side view of his or her face) to represent that character. Trace it with thick black marker and cut it out. Make sure you include the neck of the character.

3 Label the top (crown) "*character's name* Versus Himself/Herself." Write the title of the book and the author's name at the bottom, in the neck area.

4 Fill in the rest of the silhouette with a description of the conflict and the character's attempts to solve it. Finish with the final resolution.

Grading Criteria

Silhouette accurately describes the conflict the character had within him or herself.	20 Points
Silhouette describes attempts to resolve conflict and final resolution.	20 Points
Neatness	5 Points
Mechanics	5 Points
	50 Points

Pictorial Representation

Conflict

Skill: Describe a person-versus-nature conflict.

What you'll need:

construction paper, scissors, glue, and markers

Steps:

1 In a person-versus-nature conflict, a character is challenged by his or her environment: weather, terrain, time, geography, and so on. Use construction paper and other art supplies to create a pictorial representation of the natural element with which the main character from the book you've read struggled.

2 Write a description of the conflict in an area of the element and the outcome in another. For example, if the character struggled to survive a thunderstorm, you might draw and cut out a big cloud and glue lightning strikes to the bottom of it. Then you would describe the conflict inside the cloud and the outcome on the lightning strikes.

3 Make sure to include on your drawing the title of the book, the author's name, and your title: "*character's name* Versus *natural element*."

Grading Criteria

Natural element created is appropriate to the conflict in the story.	15 Points
Description of the conflict and the outcome is detailed and well written.	15 Points
Creativity	10 Points
Neatness	5 Points
Mechanics	5 Points
	50 Points

Evaluation Grid

Skill: Describe a person-versus-society conflict.
Create and evaluate alternative solutions.

Conflict

Evaluation Grid (page 89) and a sheet of notebook paper

Steps:

1 In a person-versus-society conflict, a character struggles against an accepted practice of the society, such as an injustice, oppression, or unfairness. Think about how a character in the story you've read was treated fairly or unfairly by society.

2 Use the grid to complete the following assignment. Briefly describe the conflict on the line above the grid (for example, "juvenile crime"). In the first Creative Ideas box (top row) write the specific event or action that shows how the character was treated by society (for example, "sent to Camp Green Lake"). Across the top of the grid, add some other creative ways of how that character could have been treated. Down the left-hand column list five criteria to help you judge the action or event (for example, easy to do, lasting effect, cost, everyone agrees, legal, fair to everyone involved, safe to do). Then evaluate each idea against the criteria you came up with by ranking them from 1 to 5 (with a score of 1 the worst and 5 the best).

3 Add up your scores. The idea that has the highest score is the best solution to your problem. Explain this idea (the way that character should have been treated or punished by society) in detail on the lines provided.

Grading Criteria

Grid shows four new ways that the character could have been treated or punished.	15 Points
Evaluation criteria are appropriate to problem at hand.	15 Points
Written description clearly explains new way to resolve conflict.	15 Points
Mechanics	5 Points
	50 Points

Name: _Carmen_   Date: _November 12_

EVALUATION GRID

Person-versus-society conflict: _Stanley vs. Society (juvenile crime-theft)_

Evaluation Criteria \ Creative Ideas	Send to Camp Green Lake	jail sentence	community service	house arrest	pay fine in the amount of the shoes cost
safe	2	1	5	5	5
legal	2	5	5	5	5
cost	4	2	5	4	1
lasting effect on Stanley	5	3	4	4	3
Easy to do	3	4	4	3	1
Total Points	16	15	(23)	21	15

Rating System

5 Points: excellent idea
4 Points: good idea
3 Points: average idea
2 Points: below-average idea
1 Point: poor idea

The way the character should have been treated by society is _to sentence him to a year of community service._ because _that way Stanley would be punished and the community wins because he can clean up streets and make his town look nicer and no one gets hurt._

Acrostic Poem

Skill: Describe a person-versus-machine conflict.

What you'll need:

a sheet of white 8 1/2- by 11-inch copy paper and markers

Steps:

1 In a person-versus-machine conflict, a character struggles against a machine or tool. Think about the machine a character struggles with in the book you've read and create an acrostic poem using the name of the machine. (An acrostic is a poem that sets the letters of a word in a vertical column. Each letter begins a line of the poem.) For example, if a character in your story is working on a huge research paper and the computer deletes her whole report, you might write the word "computer" down the left side of your paper and describe that conflict in the lines of the poem.

2 Fill in each line so that the entire acrostic describes the conflict the character had with this machine. Put a colorful, decorative border around your poem that relates to the conflict.

Grading Criteria

Conflict of person-versus-machine and the end result is described through the poem.	20 Points
Poem follows acrostic pattern.	10 Points
Decorative border relates to the conflict.	10 Points
Mechanics	5 Points
Creativity	5 Points
	50 Points

Question Mark

Skill: Describe a person-versus-the-unknown conflict.

What you'll need:

Question Mark (page 90)

Steps:

1 In a person-versus-the unknown conflict, a character struggles against an unknown force. For example, a character may be scared by strange noises he hears in the attic. Choose an incident in the book in which a character struggles against an unknown force.

2 Describe that conflict and its outcome in detail inside the question-mark shape.

3 Inside the dot at the bottom of the question mark, write the title of the book, the author's name, and the conflict type.

Grading Criteria

Description identifies a person-versus-the-unknown conflict.	10 Points
Description of the conflict and the outcome is well written and detailed.	25 Points
Mechanics	10 Points
Neatness	5 Points
	50 Points

Bookmark

Skill: Describe a person-versus-beast conflict.

What you'll need:

a sheet of oaktag (cut into a 2- by 5-inch piece) and markers

Steps:

1 In a person-versus-beast conflict, a character struggles against a real or imaginary beast. Many fairy tales, such as *Little Red Riding Hood*, feature this type of conflict. Choose an incident in the book you've read that shows a character struggling against an animal or other creature.

2 Use the oaktag strip to create a bookmark that illustrates this type of conflict.

3 On the front of the bookmark write the title of the book and the author's name, draw a colorful illustration of the conflict, and label it "*character's name* Versus *type of beast*."

4 On the back of your bookmark, describe the conflict and the outcome of the conflict in detail.

Grading Criteria

Front and back of bookmark follow directions in Step 2.	10 Points
Description identifies a person-versus-beast conflict.	10 Points
Description of the conflict and the outcome is well written and detailed.	20 Points
Creativity	5 Points
Mechanics	5 Points
	50 Points

Analyze This!

Skill: Identify several conflict types.

What you'll need:

Analyze This! Chart (page 91), Conflict Types (page 88)

Steps:

1 After you have finished reading, think about the many different conflicts that occurred in your story. (Refer to Conflict Types for an explanation of each type of conflict.)

2 Using the three most important conflicts in the story, fill in the chart. Be sure to accurately describe the conflict type, the problem the character faced, and how the conflict was resolved.

Grading Criteria

Problem is explained accurately.	15 Points
Conflict type matches problem.	10 Points
Conflict resolution is described accurately.	15 Points
Neatness	5 Points
Mechanics	5 Points
	50 Points

Prove It!

Skill: Find evidence of different types of conflict in a story.

What you'll need:

Prove It! Chart (page 92)

Steps:

❶ Identify as many types of conflict as you can in the book you've read.

❷ Prove that you have found a conflict type by listing evidence, such as quotes, sentences, phrases, and words, in the right-hand column of the chart.

❸ If you find more than one example of a type of conflict, such as two person-versus-self conflicts, list evidence for both of them in the right-hand column.

Grading Criteria

Each type of conflict is identified correctly.	20 Points
Adequate proof is given.	20 Points
Neatness	5 points
Mechanics	5 Points
	50 Points

Name: _____ Date: _____

PROVE IT! CHART

Title: ___The Most Dangerous Game_____

Author: ____Richard Connell_____

CONFLICT TYPE	EVIDENCE
Person Versus Person Rainsford –vs- Zaroff	The hunt that lasted several days and ended in Zaroff's demise.
Person Versus Self- Rainsford –vs- Physical Limitations	Rainsford fighting his own physical limitations in the water and during the hunt.
Person Versus Nature Rainsford –vs- the Jungle	Rainsford must fight through the overgrown jungle he is not familiar with.
Person Versus Machine Ivan –vs- the Knife	The Ugandian trick Rainsford learned to attach a knife to a springy sapling killed Zaroff's servant, Ivan.
Person Versus Society Zaroff –vs- Societal Values	Zaroff's believes it is perfectly fine to hunt and kill humans for the pleasure and the challenge of the hunt.
Person Versus Unknown Rainsford –vs- the Island	Rainsford's ability to hide and survive Zaroff hunting him on the unknown ShipTrap Island.
Person Versus Beast Rainsford –vs- Zaroff's Dogs	Rainsford's Burmese tiger pit he constructed to kill Zaroff, killed one of Zaroff's best dogs.

92   *Independent Reading Management Kit: Literary Elements* SCHOLASTIC TEACHING RESOURCES

Name: _____ Date: _____

CONFLICT TYPES

PERSON VERSUS PERSON

A struggle between two characters.

Example: A girl dares another girl to steal something.

PERSON VERSUS SELF

A character's struggle against his or her own emotions, conscience, or physical abilities.

Example: A teen struggles over whether to report a classmate he saw cheating.

PERSON VERSUS NATURE

A character's struggle against weather, environment, time, geography, etc.

Example: A man's house is blown away in a hurricane.

PERSON VERSUS MACHINE

A character's struggle against a machine or tool.

Example: A computer deletes your entire report.

PERSON VERSUS SOCIETY

A character's struggle against some societal or institutional injustice, oppression, unfairness, etc.

"Justice Now!"

Example: A convicted man appeals a jury's verdict he feels is unfair.

PERSON VERSUS UNKNOWN

A character's struggle against an unknown force.

Example: He was scared by the strange noises he heard in the attic.

PERSON VERSUS BEAST

A character's struggle against a real or imaginary creature.

Example: A prince goes to fight an evil dragon to win the heart of the princess.

Independent Reading Management Kit: Literary Elements SCHOLASTIC TEACHING RESOURCES

Name: _____ Date: _____

EVALUATION GRID

Person-versus-society conflict: _____

Evaluation Criteria \ Creative Ideas					
Total Points					

Rating System
5 Points: excellent idea
4 Points: good idea
3 Points: average idea
2 Points: below-average idea
1 Point: poor idea

The way the character should have been treated by society is _____

_____

because_____

_____

_____

_____

QUESTION MARK

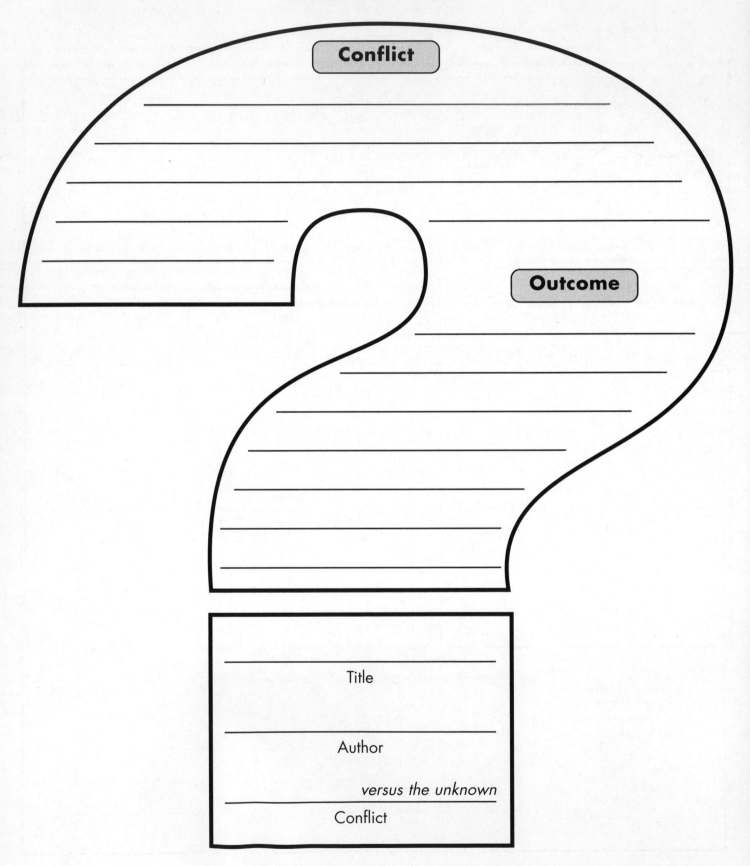

Conflict

Outcome

Title

Author

versus the unknown

Conflict

Independent Reading Management Kit: Literary Elements   SCHOLASTIC TEACHING RESOURCES

Name: _____ Date: _____

ANALYZE THIS! CHART

Book Title: _____

	Conflict Type	Problem	Result
1			
2			
3			

Name: _____ Date: _____

PROVE IT! CHART

Title: _____

Author: _____

CONFLICT TYPE	EVIDENCE
Person Versus Person	
Person Versus Self	
Person Versus Nature	
Person Versus Machine	
Person Versus Society	
Person Versus Unknown	
Person Versus Beast	

Independent Reading Management Kit: Literary Elements   SCHOLASTIC TEACHING RESOURCES

Name: _____ Date: _____

GRADING SUMMARY

	Possible Score:	My Score:

☐ **Sandwich Board**

Conflict described is person versus person. — 10 Points _____

Conflict is written in detail from each character's perspective. — 20 Points _____

Sandwich board contains colorful illustrations that reflect the conflict from different perspectives. — 15 Points _____

Neatness — 5 Points _____

50 Points _____

☐ **Silhouette**

Silhouette accurately describes the conflict the character had within him or herself. — 20 Points _____

Silhouette describes attempts to resolve conflict and final resolution. — 20 Points _____

Neatness — 5 Points _____

Mechanics — 5 Points _____

50 Points _____

☐ **Pictorial Representation**

Natural element created is appropriate to the conflict in the story. — 15 Points _____

Description of the conflict and the outcome is detailed and well written. — 15 Points _____

Creativity — 10 Points _____

Neatness — 5 Points _____

Mechanics — 5 Points _____

50 Points _____

☐ **Evaluation Grid**

Grid shows four new ways that the character could have been treated or punished. — 15 Points _____

Evaluation criteria are appropriate to problem at hand. — 15 Points _____

Written description clearly explains new way to resolve conflict. — 15 Points _____

Mechanics — 5 Points _____

50 Points _____

☐ Acrostic Poem

Conflict of person-versus-machine and the end result is
described through the poem.   20 Points _____

Poem follows acrostic pattern.   10 Points _____

Decorative border relates to the conflict.   10 Points _____

Mechanics   5 Points _____

Creativity   5 Points _____

                                                               50 Points _____

☐ Question Mark

Description identifies a person-versus-the-unknown conflict.   10 Points _____

Description of the conflict and the outcome is well written
and detailed.   25 Points _____

Mechanics   10 Points _____

Neatness   5 Points _____

                                                               50 Points _____

☐ Bookmark

Front and back of bookmark follow directions in Step 2.   10 Points _____

Description identifies a person-versus-beast conflict.   10 Points _____

Description of the conflict and the outcome is well written and detailed. 20 Points _____

Creativity   5 Points _____

Mechanics   5 Points _____

                                                              50 Points _____

☐ Analyze This!

Problem is explained accurately.   15 Points _____

Conflict type matches problem.   10 Points _____

Conflict resolution is described accurately.   15 Points _____

Neatness   5 Points _____

Mechanics   5 Points _____

                                                            50 Points _____

☐ Prove It!

Each type of conflict is identified correctly.   20 Points _____

Adequate proof is given.   20 Points _____

Neatness   5 points _____

Mechanics   5 Points _____

                                                           50 Points _____

Total for all three projects _____

Independent Reading Management Kit: Literary Elements   SCHOLASTIC TEACHING RESOURCES

Author's Style Projects

Name: _____ Due Date: _____

Book Title: _____

Tongue Twisters	**Charm Bracelet**	**Identify and Illustrate**
Ballad	**Flip Book**	**Spinners**
Chart	**Picture Book**	**Letter to the Author**

We could hear the hungry, low growl of the storm, prowling behind Big Mountain...

Tongue Twisters

Skill: Use alliteration to describe a book.

What you'll need:

the picture book Animalia by Graeme Base, four sheets of white copy paper, colored pencils, stapler

Steps:

1 Alliteration is the repeated use of the same sound at the beginning of each word in a sentence or phrase. Authors of Read Aloud books sometimes use this playful, tongue-twisting technique. Read the book *Animalia* by Graeme Base. This book gives a descriptive, alliterative phrase for each letter of the alphabet. Using the ABC book format and the alliterative style of Graeme Base, write a description of the book you've read.

2 Set up your ABC book by stacking together and folding four sheets of white paper in half so that the pages open like a book. Staple three times along the fold to keep the book together.

3 Design a cover for your book that includes the title of the book you've read: "*title of book* Tongue Twisters" (e.g., "*Shiloh* Tongue Twisters"). Also include the name of the author, your name, and a colorful illustration related to the theme of the book.

4 Begin writing your book on page 3, fitting text and illustrations for two letters of the alphabet on each page. For each letter, write an alliterative sentence, using information or ideas from the book you've read and draw a colorful illustration to match the sentence.

Grading Criteria

ABC book uses alliterative style of Graeme Base.	15 Points
ABC book is filled with information from the novel.	15 Points
Illustrations relate to alliterative sentences.	10 Points
Creativity	5 Points
Mechanics	5 Points
	50 Points

Charm Bracelet

Skill: Identify symbolism.

What you'll need:

Charm Bracelet (page 103), markers or colored pencils

Steps:

1 Charm bracelets are extremely popular these days. The charms people wear on their bracelets symbolize events in their lives that are special to them.

2 Design a charm bracelet for the book you've read. Draw and color seven charms on the Charm Bracelet sheet to symbolize important parts of the book. Next to each charm, explain what it symbolizes in the story. Note: You may create drawings for symbols that appear in the book (e.g. an empty chair for loneliness) or create your own symbols for important elements like setting, character, conflict , and theme.

Grading Criteria

All seven charms appropriately symbolize the book read.	15 Points
Written description of charm explains the symbolism.	15 Points
All charms are neat and colorful.	10 Points
Creativity	10 Points
	50 Points

Identify and Illustrate

Skill: Identify and illustrate similes from a story.

What you'll need:

three sheets of construction paper, markers or colored pencils

Steps:

1 A simile is a descriptive technique in which an author uses *like* or *as* to compare two unlike things. One element helps describe the other, as in *The Great Dane was as big as a house.* (*House* shows how big the dog is). Find sentences in the text of the book you've read (or create three descriptive sentences about the book) that contain similes.

2 Write and illustrate each sentence on a sheet of construction paper.

3 For each example write which two objects are being compared and what the simile actually means. If you found the simile in the book, cite the page number for reference.

Grading Criteria	
Sentences chosen each contain a simile.	10 Points
Illustrations are colorful and relate to the simile.	10 Points
Comparisons made are appropriate.	10 Points
Similes make sense.	10 Points
Page number where simile was found is included.	5 Points
Mechanics	5 Points
	50 Points

Ballad

Skill: Use rhyme to create a ballad that comments on a character.

What you'll need:

a sheet of white copy paper and markers

Steps:

1 A ballad is a popular kind of narrative poem, adapted for recitation or singing—it's a song that tells a story. Think about a character from the book you've read about whom you can create a ballad. Make sure to pick a character you know well.

2 The ballad that you create must include a title, rhyming verses, and five or more stanzas. Also, the lyrics must reveal what happened to this character throughout the story and tell about his or her life as you know it through your reading.

3 Write a final draft of the ballad on white copy paper in pen or type, and draw a decorative border around it to match the theme of the book.

4 Read or perform your ballad to the class.

Grading Criteria	
Ballad tells about the life of a character from the story accurately.	15 Points
Ballad has five or more stanzas and rhyming verses.	15 Points
Decorative border complements the story.	10 Points
Creativity	10 Points
	50 Points

Flip Book

Skill: Create a metaphor based on events in the story.

What you'll need:

Flip Book Forms sheets (pages 104–106), markers or colored pencils

Grading Criteria

Metaphors created are appropriate for the story elements listed in Step 2.   15 Points

An appropriate color illustration accompanies each metaphor. 15 Points

Sentences created are metaphors.   10 Points

Creativity   5 Points

Neatness   5 Points
_____
50 Points

Steps:

1 A metaphor is a way of describing something by calling it something else. Unlike a simile, a metaphor makes a direct comparison: *The Great Dane was a house.*

2 Make up a metaphor for each of the following in the book you've read: the setting, two different characters, the problem in the story, and the solution. Each metaphor must reflect important ideas and events in your story.

3 Follow these directions to create the flip book:

 a. Fold each form on the dashed line.

 b. Place form 2 inside form 1.

 c. Place form 3 inside form 2.

 d. Staple the forms together along the fold.

 e. On each page of the flip book write the name of a story element listed in Step 2.

 f. Next to the story element, write the metaphor you created. Lift the flap and draw a colorful illustration for it in the blank space above. In this way, readers will first encounter your written metaphor and then flip up the flap to find the illustration.

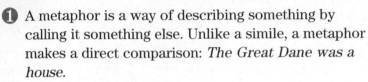

98   *Independent Reading Management Kit: Literary Elements*

Spinners

Skill: Use personification to respond to literature.

What you'll need:

three copies of Spinner Circle Template (page 107), Personification Chart (page 108), hole puncher, curling ribbon (any color), glue, markers or colored pencils

Steps:

Grading Criteria

Sentences contain inventive personifications with key elements from the book.	15 Points
Illustrations complement personified sentences.	10 Points
Spinner is made and decorated according to directions on template.	10 Points
Creativity	10 Points
Neatness	5 Points
	50 Points

❶ Personification is a literary technique that gives human qualities to ideas or nonliving things. (*Courage strode tall and proud through the locker room. The rock sat miserably alone through the long winter.*)

❷ Use the chart to help you write ten inventive sentences with personification that describe the book you've read. Start with an inanimate object or idea from the story in the first row (*rock*), add a human characteristic in the second row (*loneliness*), and give descriptive details to paint a picture in the third row (*miserably alone, sat, long winter*). Then write your sentence in the fourth row.

❸ Pick your favorite three sentences and write each on a circle template.

❹ Illustrate the personified sentences in the area of the circle above the sentence lines.

❺ Create a decorative border around each circle that complements your personified sentence.

❻ Follow the directions on your circle template to create a 3-D spinner. Hole-punch the top, lace a curling ribbon through the hole, and find a place to hang your spinner so it can be read from different directions.

Chart

Skill: Use imagery to respond to literature.

What you'll need:

ruler, pencil, white copy paper

Steps:

1 Use a ruler, pencil, and paper or the "draw table" function on a word processing program to create a chart with the five senses at the top of each column: "Looks Like," "Tastes Like," "Sounds Like," "Smells Like," and "Feels Like" and ten rows. Choose ten different elements from the book you've read, such as characters, places, and objects, that you feel could use more description.

2 Your task is to list those ten elements on the chart and fill in the columns with adjectives (describing words) to make the elements more vivid and easy to imagine. Include one or two adjectives for each of the senses.

3 On the back of your chart make an image-filled sentence for each item that uses some or all of the words you came up with.

Grading Criteria

Chart lists ten elements from the story.	5 Points
Words listed in chart describe the elements and relate to all the senses.	20 points
Sentences use sensory words from chart to create vivid images.	20 Points
Creativity	5 Points
	50 Points

IMAGERY CHART — Ross

SENSES: / CHOICES:	Looks Like	Tastes Like	Sounds Like	Smells Like	Feels Like
1. Rock	• Gray	• Dirt	• Thunder	• Moss	• Hard
2. Bessie, Miss	• Cow	• Halbeef	• Mooing	• Cow Pies/Hay	• Strong/Meaty
3. Mrs. Myers	• Old Woman	• N/A	• Nagging	• Chalk/Pencil Shavings	• Rough Skin
4. Bill Burke	• Middle-Aged	• N/A	• Typing Keys	• Fresh Ink	• Smooth Hands
5. Mr. Arrons	• Hard-Working	• N/A	• The Pickup Motor	• Sweat	• Tough
6. Prince Terrien	• Little/Brown+Black	• N/A	• Little Barks + Yelps	• The Outdoors	• Soft
7. Gary Fulcher	• A Boy	• NA	• Insults	• Hair Gel	• Weak
8. Leslie Burke	• Short, Shaggy, Brown Hair	• N/A	• Happy	• Perfume	• Soft Skin
9. Janice Avery	• Big	• N/A	• Mean	• Cheap Perfume	• Fat Rolls
10. Miss Edmunds	• Attractive	• N/A	• Wonderful Music	• Flowers	• Gentle

"BRIDGE TO TERABITHIA"

1) The smell of moss arose when the hard, gray rock fell to the dirt like thunder.

2) Miss Bessie, the cow, was mooing when her strong leg stepped in a cowpie.

3) People hated Mrs. Myers because she was an old woman with rough skin, smelled like chalk, + was always nagging.

4) Bill Burke's smooth hands always smelled of fresh ink, now that he was middle-aged.

5) Mr. Arrons is a tough, hard-working man, but he smells like sweat.

6) Prince Terrien's soft, brown + black fur smelled of the outdoors.

7) Gary Fulcher is a weak boy who smells like hair gel + insults people a lot.

8) Leslie Burke is always happy even though she has short, brown, shaggy hair.

9) Janice Avery is a big, mean girl who puts cheap perfume on her fat rolls.

10) Miss Edmunds is a gentle + attractive woman who smells like flowers + plays wonderful music.

Picture Book

Skill: Use repetition, a powerful literary technique.

What you'll need:

the picture book *Brown Bear, Brown Bear, What Do You See?* by Bill Martin, three sheets of white copy paper, stapler, crayons, markers or colored pencils

Steps:

1 Read *Brown Bear, Brown Bear, What Do You See?* and pay special attention to Bill Martin's use of repetition and how it makes his writing effective.

2 Using ideas and events from the book you've read and your understanding of Martin's style, create your own picture book. Here's how:

a. Stack and then fold three sheets of copy paper in half to make a twelve-page booklet and staple three times at the fold.

b. Make a cover on the front page. On the cover, write a new title that includes the main character and reads like Martin's title. For example, if the book you've read is *Holes* by Louis Sachar, your new title may be *Stanley, Stanley, What Do You See?* The cover also needs to say "adapted from *the title of the book you've read*." Add a colorful illustration to match the title.

c. Leave page 2 blank and begin writing your book on page 3. On pages 3–12 write a series of sentences that lead from one to the next, following Bill Martin's pattern. (See example below.) As you write, make sure that everyone or everything in your picture book "sees" events or things mentioned in the book you've read. Continue this repetitive pattern throughout your picture book.

d. Illustrate each page.

e. On the back of your picture book, write a paragraph explaining what effect the repetition had on your writing. Was it effective or not?

Grading Criteria

Repetition is used effectively.	10 Points
Picture book is based on ideas and events from the book you've read.	10 Points
Illustrations in picture book are colorful and help tell the story.	10 Points
Paragraph on back cover explains whether repetition is effective or ineffective.	10 Points
Followed directions to create the book.	5 Points
Creativity	5 Points
	50 Points

Letter to the Author

Skill: Evaluate the effectiveness of various stylistic techniques used by an author.

What you'll need:

Common Style Techniques (page 109), lined paper or white copy paper

Steps:

1 Think about the various elements of style used by the author of the book you've read. For a refresher on different styles an author may use, refer to Common Style Techniques.

2 Write a letter to the author telling him or her which book you've read. In your letter, comment on whether or not you liked the book, the various style techniques he or she used, and whether or not they were effective. Use examples, including quotes and sentences from the book, to support your opinion. For example, you may note that the author included too much imagery, or that flashbacks were hard to follow, or that the author's great use of hyperbole made the book humorous.

3 Write or type the final draft in a business-letter format (you may use the business-letter format in your computer's word processing program). Include a heading with your address and the date, the inside address (the author's name and complete address), an appropriate greeting, a polite closing, and your signature. You may need to do some research to find the author's address. If you can't locate it, make up one that would be appropriate, given what you have learned about the author.

Your street address
City, state, zip code

Month and day, year

Author's name
Street address
City, state, zip code

Dear Mr./Ms._____,

This is the body of the letter. Describe the book you've read and give the author constructive feedback by evaluating the author's style. Use examples from the book to support your opinion.

Remember to skip spaces between paragraphs. There is no need to indent. Each line begins at the left margin.

Sincerely,
Your name

Name: _____ Date: _____

CHARM BRACELET

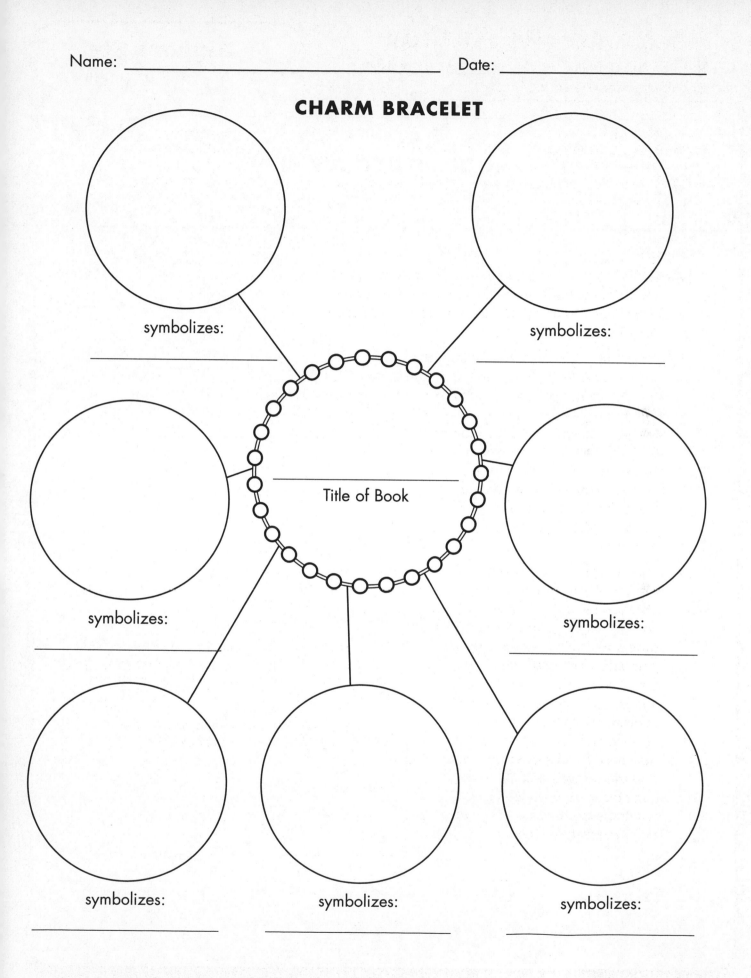

symbolizes:

_____

symbolizes:

_____

Title of Book

symbolizes:

_____

symbolizes:

_____

symbolizes:

_____

symbolizes:

_____

symbolizes:

_____

Author: _____

Book Title: _____

METAPHOR FLIP BOOK

Form 1

Form 2

Form 3

Name: _____ Date: _____

SPINNER CIRCLE TEMPLATE

Directions:

1. Start with three copies of this template.

2. Fill in and decorate the three spinner circles following the activity directions (Steps 3–5).

3. Cut out the circles and fold them each in half using the dotted line as a guide.

4. Put the circles together with the folded edge facing in to the center and the decorated sides facing out. This creates a 3-D globe. Glue the backsides of the three circles together, so that each circle is connected to the other two circles.

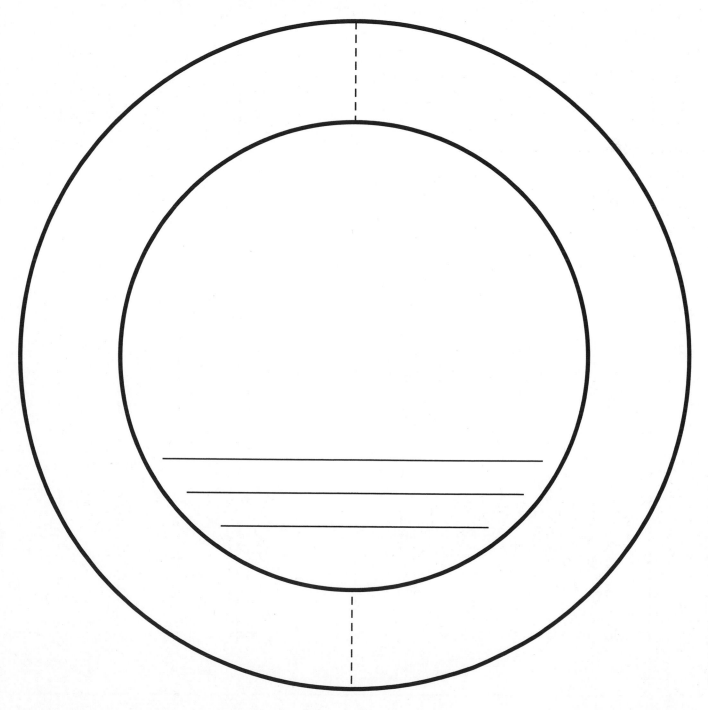

Name: _____ Date: _____

PERSONIFICATION CHART

Object or Idea	Humanistic Characteristic	Details	Sentence
1.			
2.			
3.			
4.			
5.			
6.			
7.			
8.			
9.			
10.			

Independent Reading Management Kit: Literary Elements   SCHOLASTIC TEACHING RESOURCES

COMMON STYLE TECHNIQUES

AUTHOR'S STYLE: The way an author expresses him or herself with word choice, sentence structure, and language. Just as we all have a style of dressing, so each author has a distinctive writing style. An author's style affects how we read and react to his or her story. Here are some common techniques.

Alliteration: Grouping together two or more words that repeat the same sound.
Ex. *An awesome aardvark advances across the avenue awkwardly.*

Flashback: An interruption in the chronological plot sequence to present an earlier scene or episode.
Ex. *As the woman sat at the window watching the children load the school bus, she remembered her first time riding a school bus many years ago.*

Foreshadowing: Providing hints about what may happen later in the story line.
Ex. *Alexa cringed when the substitute nervously wrote on the board: "Ms. Topaz will be absent indefinitely."*

Hyperbole: An obvious exaggeration that is not meant to be taken literally. Often used in humorous writing.
Ex. *This book weighs a ton.*

Imagery: Descriptive language that appeals to the senses (sight, sound, smell, touch, and taste).
Ex. The snowflake glistened diamond-bright in the sun.

Irony: A way of writing that means the opposite of what the words say; the opposite of what is expected.
Ex. *A police officer gets a speeding ticket.*

Metaphor: A figure of speech in which one thing is called another to highlight a special feature.
Ex. *The still lake was a cathedral.*

Onomatopoeia: Words that sound like the thing they stand for.
Ex. *buzz, whoosh, beep*

Personification: Giving human qualities to ideas or inanimate objects.
Ex. *The sun smiled down on us.*

Repetition: The use of the same word or phrase several times for emphasis.
Ex. *"Ainsley, Ainsley, Ainsley! How many times do I have to tell you to clean your room?"*

Rhyme: The use of words that have similar sounds in a poem or verse.
Ex. *Cloud and sky/ Wet and dry* (Karla Kuskin)

Satire: Writing that makes fun of people's ideas or ways of doing things.
Ex. *The movie "Shrek" satirizes many familiar fairy tales, such as Robin Hood.*

Simile: A figure of speech in which one thing is compared with another using the words *like* or *as*.
Ex. *The stale bread was as hard as a rock.*

Symbolism: The use of an object or idea to represent something other than itself.
Ex. *A dove may symbolize peace.*

Tone: The author's attitude toward his or her subject and audience.
Ex. *Ask yourself, is the author involved or detached from the subject? How does he or she feel? Is he or she joking, serious, approving, angry?*

Name: _____ Date: _____

GRADING SUMMARY

	Possible Score:	My Score:

☐ **Tongue Twisters**

ABC book uses alliterative style of Graeme Base.	15 Points	_____
ABC book is filled with information from the novel.	15 Points	_____
Illustrations relate to alliterative sentences.	10 Points	_____
Creativity	5 Points	_____
Mechanics	5 Points	_____
	50 Points	_____

☐ **Charm Bracelet**

All seven charms appropriately symbolize the book read.	15 Points	_____
Written description of charm explains the symbolism.	15 Points	_____
All charms are neat and colorful.	10 Points	_____
Creativity	10 Points	_____
	50 Points	_____

☐ **Identify and Illustrate**

Sentences chosen each contain a simile.	10 Points	_____
Illustration is colorful and relates to the simile.	10 Points	_____
Comparisons made are appropriate.	10 Points	_____
Similes make sense.	10 Points	_____
Page number where simile was found is included.	5 Points	_____
Mechanics	5 Points	_____
	50 Points	_____

☐ **Flip Book**

Metaphors created are appropriate for the story elements listed in Step 2.	15 Points	_____
An appropriate color illustration accompanies each metaphor.	15 Points	_____
Sentences created are metaphors.	10 Points	_____
Creativity	5 Points	_____
Neatness	5 Points	_____
	50 Points	_____

☐ Ballad

Ballad tells about the life of one character from the story accurately.	15 Points	_____
Ballad has five or more stanzas and rhyming verses.	15 Points	_____
Decorative border complements the story.	10 Points	_____
Creativity	10 Points	_____
	50 Points	_____

☐ Spinners

Sentences contain inventive personifications with key elements from the book.	15 Points	_____
Illustrations complement personified sentences.	10 Points	_____
Spinner is made and decorated according to directions on template.	10 Points	_____
Creativity	10 Points	_____
Neatness	5 Points	_____
	50 Points	_____

☐ Chart

Chart lists 10 elements from the story.	5 Points	_____
Words listed in chart describe the elements and relate to all the senses.	20 points	_____
Sentences use sensory words from chart to create vivid images.	20 Points	_____
Creativity	5 Points	_____
	50 Points	_____

☐ Picture Book

Repetition is used effectively.	10 Points	_____
Picture book is based on ideas and events from the book you've read.	10 Points	_____
Illustrations in picture book are colorful and help tell the story.	10 Points	_____
Paragraph on back cover explains whether repetition is effective or ineffective.	10 Points	_____
Followed directions to create the book.	5 Points	_____
Creativity	5 Points	_____
	50 Points	_____

☐ Letter to the Author

Letter effectively comments on the stylistic techniques used by the author.	10 Points	_____
Letter discusses the effectiveness of the techniques.	10 Points	_____
Letter uses examples from the book to back up opinion.	15 Points	_____
Letter is written in a professional tone.	10 Points	_____
Mechanics	5 Points	_____
	50 Points	_____

Total for all three projects _____

Think-Tac-Toe Template

Name: _____   Due Date: _____

Book Title: _____

Independent Reading Management Kit: Literary Elements   SCHOLASTIC TEACHING RESOURCES